Through the Tunnel

A TRAVELER'S GUIDE TO SPIRITUAL REBIRTH

Diane Goble, M.S.

S.O.U.L. Foundation, Inc. • Palm Harbor, Florida USA

Through the Tunnel

A TRAVELER'S GUIDE TO SPIRITUAL REBIRTH

Published and distributed by:
S.O.U.L. Foundation, Inc.
P.O. Box 6141
Palm Harbor, FL 34684-0741

Library of Congress Card Catalog Number 93-86052

ISBN 0-9638606-0-7

Printed on Recycled Paper

Manufactured in the United States of America

Acknowledgement

I am indebted to the many authors who have written about death and dying before me, who have helped bring this subject out in the open, especially Elisabeth Kubler-Ross, Ray Moody, Ken Ring and Earlyne Chaney.

I am deeply grateful to my sister, JoAnn, and her husband, Gary Chambers, for their love and support -- to JoAnn for her beautiful type design for the book; to Gary for his gift of heavenly music to sooth my scattered psyche. And to my mother, Anne Mecouch, for her proofreading abilities and for her love and support, in spite of her doubts.

I wish to thank the friends who helped me produce this book: June Bletzer for her definitions, Gary Young for typesetting services, Liz LaJoy for the cover photography, Ross Brandt for cover computer graphics and my spiritual guides and master teachers, who kept me on track long enough to finish this book.

And, most of all, I am grateful to Mother-Father-God for the opportunity to go through the tunnel, visit the spiritual world, and return with the mission of sharing my experiences with others so they may prepare themselves for their own journey through the tunnel and beyond.

Do not stand by my grave and weep.

I am not there, I do not sleep.

I am a thousand winds that blow.

I am a diamond glint of snow.

I am the sunlight on ripened grain.

I am the gentle autumn rain.

When you awake in the morning hush,

I am the swift, uplifting rush

Of quiet birds in circling flights.

I am the soft starshine at night.

Do not stand by my grave and cry.

I am not there . . . I did not die.

Author Unknown

Travelogue

Introduction

My joy comes from sharing the Good News that 90% of the things people worry about are not worth the time or the energy they put into them. The Big Picture is that "life" as a Human Being is a *learning* experience that does <u>not</u> end when the physical body dies, and is only a <u>brief</u> episode in the infinite life of a <u>much</u> greater being who is both Human <u>and</u> Divine. Not GOD, but a great Spiritual Master. Human Beings are the physical manifestation of a Spiritual Being who is on a Path back to the Ultimate Reality, the Godhead. Life's little dramas are meaningless distractions from our higher purpose.

The only thing that <u>really</u> matters in our physical lifetimes is that we learn to reflect God's Love, or the Christ-Spirit, in our daily lives by balancing the Physical-Emotional-Mental-Spiritual Nature of our Whole Being. It is the atomic balanced with the Cosmic. *As it is above; so it is below!* We are waves of light and we are particles of light. We are learning to *simultaneously* exist on all levels as fully-awakened, God-like Beings.

It will take many "lifetimes" in the physical dimension for one of a Soul's human "children" to grasp the full meaning of the preceding concept and to accept that each of us is Divine and has equal rights in all earthly matters, before one of those children reaches that one final lifetime as a fully-realized Divine-Human Being. Not as a saint or a martyr, but as an ordinary person who loves and helps others and enjoys living, no matter what the circumstances of their physical life. And, when <u>that</u> physical life is over, the Spirit no longer needs or wants to project into the world of matter — has graduated from the School of Life — and seeks greater knowledge and wisdom in the higher dimensions of GOD. It is our greater developmental process and you and I are in the midst of ours!

Each of us is given the opportunity to accelerate our spiritual growth by expanding our consciousness to accept the down-pouring of God's Love (to accept a spiritual teacher to guide you, if that is what it takes for you) and by opening our hearts to that healing energy of unconditional Love and Acceptance. I wish I could find the words to convey what I felt during my near-death experience (NDE) to help you relate to the overwhelming feeling that swept over me after leaving my body and while traveling through spiritual dimensions at the speed of light. Try to imagine the most intense feeling of being loved that you can and multiply it by the National Debt, and you'd have some inkling of what it is like when you are able to let go of the physical world and experience higher states of consciousness in the less-dense spiritual worlds beyond the physical dimension.

Skeptics may call a description by an NDEr a hallucination brought on by oxygen deprivation, but, for the individual, the intense feeling of complete Love, the mind-expanding realizations of the multi-dimensional universe and the continuity of conscious-life, and the life-transforming effects on the person following an NDE, is less easily explained away . . . though Science may never find convincing evidence. The veil between the physical and the spiritual dimension cannot be penetrated by our limited physical senses. It is only when the Conscious Mind leaves the body-brain (during NDEs, out-of-body-experiences, trance and dream states) and joins its Astral body that we can perceive our environment in the spiritual realms— and it is very much, and more, like the physical.

At the time of my NDE I considered myself an atheist and had no expectations of anything beyond death. But, in an instant, I changed my mind! And I didn't just believe something, I "knew" it from first-hand experience. In fact, it felt more real and natural than this world ever has, before or since. Now that I know so many others have had a similar experience, I feel safe in coming out of the closet, even though many people around me don't want to hear about death or can't imagine looking forward to it.

The message I was given is that it is time to make death a <u>part</u> of life and not the <u>end</u> of life. We need to talk about it, get comfortable with it, and we need to prepare ourselves and our loved ones for our departure, as well as our reunion at the end of their physical lives... for we do meet again, many times, in many places.

And so, I offer this knowledge, which I brought back from my NDE and is corroborated by many others, as a contribution to world peace. It is my hope that, by recognizing we are all here to help each other along our spiritual paths, we will turn our attention away from our ego-centered desires and fears toward compassion and sharing and caring for each other. There are a lot of things to do on this planet that are meaningful and fun; why waste anymore lifetimes creating more Karma by using physical aggression against others to gain control over them or get what they have or because they are different or don't give us what we want. The karmic lesson for Humanity is concern for the welfare of generations to come, as evidenced by the state of the world today. Each of us is presented with opportunities to perform unselfish acts of love in our daily lives and with choices between right and wrong. It requires a change of mind, of attitudes and intentions, to develop one's spiritual nature, to develop the Spiritual Nature of Humanity.

Each person will comprehend the information in this book at their own level of understanding and, hopefully, each time you read it over your understanding will increase. Many Souls in body at this time will have the opportunity to make the quantum leap to higher consciousness in their present lifetime and achieve spirtual heights at their deathtime. This book is offered as a tool for those who are ready and as something to get others to start thinking "what if . . ."

Use whatever information in it that fits into your current belief system. Use it to expand your consciousness. Use it to become a more loving being. Use it to improve the quality of your life, and the lives of others, and to find joy and fulfillment in living a meaningful existence on this beautiful planet.

Whatever you do . . . I wish you love.

Paul

"What no eye has seen, nor ear heard,
nor heart of man conceived,
what God has prepared for those
who love him,
God has revealed to us through the Spirit."
(I Cor. 2:9-10)

Up the Creek Without a Paddle

We come into this world blindly, without an instruction book or any guidelines, and simply have to muddle through a lifetime as a human being without knowing who or what we are or why we're here or even where *here* is! We have parents, relatives, friends, teachers and preachers to look to as role models; history books to show us how people have lived in the past; religions to teach us the rules of living morally; governments to help us learn to live together; and the Free Will to do anything we darn well please! Somehow, amid the bitter and the sweet, the sorrow and the joy, the tears and the laughter, we get through life only to come up against death. And, once again, there is no instruction manual.

We are as unprepared to die as we were to be born. That's why death scares most people and why some stubbornly cling to life or try to ignore death. They may be more secure with what they know, no matter how miserable it may be, than with death—that Great Unknown.

A great many people today are rushed to hospitals as death approaches, and their dying becomes lonely and impersonal. They are treated as a person with no right to an opinion, as a non-person. No one asks if they want the heroic measures the doctors and nurses are determined to perform. If they rebel, they are sedated. *He may cry for rest, peace, and dignity, but he will get infusions, transfusions, a heart machine, or tracheotomy . . .* [11] Medical technology has replaced religion in the dying process and changed our attitudes about death. The dying

are isolated and deathbed rituals have been abandoned.[18]

But times are changing. Science and religion are
finding common ground and attitudes toward death
are going back to acceptance of death as part of life.
*That person is bound in the chains of death, the fears of his own
death, and the grief over the death of others, who tries to ignore
death. That person is freed from the fetters of death and all its atten-
dant anxieties, who meets death as a companion to life, in the spirit
of rational and tranquil acceptance, without clinging to or fleeing
it.*[12]

Don't waste your life fearing death! Death is simply
a change in vibrations, a rearrangement of your atomic
structure, a transformation of molecular substance, a
shift in consciousness. We are energy and, as scientists
proclaim, energy cannot be destroyed — it merely
changes form. Are not water, ice and steam all the
same thing? Your physical life and death and your spiritual rebirth are all parts of your experience. There is
no separation. After you die, you are still YOU. Everything you experience after you leave your physical body
is a continuation of your "whole" life experience. Consciousness is continuous, eternal. What you now see as
the material world, the world of ordinary sensory reality, disappears and you vanish to it as the spiritual
world, the fourth dimension, appears before you with
you in it. And you are still you.

In the fourth dimensional world, *one can view every-
thing from all angles simultaneously. The interior of a solid is as visible
as its exterior. The eyes can magnify or reduce objects according to
one's will power or desire. All objects seem to be enveloped by an
aura, constantly shifting form and color.*[5] In this realm, you will
experience having all knowledge; all past, present and
future will seem *to co-exist in a sort of timeless state.*[16]

If death is no more than part of "growing up," then all the fighting amongst, and within, ourselves is, sadly, a waste of another brief opportunity to live a lifetime as a physical being to accelerate your spiritual growth.

Once you <u>really</u> understand that death is merely a stage in the developmental process of your <u>whole</u> life, for you are both a physical <u>and</u> a spiritual entity, you can shift the focus of your present attention to exploring the potentials and opportunities your current lifetime has to offer, even if you are terminally ill. Life will not be fraught with frustration, pain, sorrow, guilt, struggle and regret if you concentrate your energy on attaining spiritual awareness and put the material world in its proper perspective. Once you can accept that death is not the end, but merely a transition from one state of being to another, that you may face temporary unpleasantness but there is no eternal damnation, and that, no matter how badly you have bungled this life, you will have other opportunities to get it right, you can overcome the fear of that Great Unknown and get on with the important questions — such as, since you know you are going to die someday, is there a right way and a wrong way to go?

Henry Ford

The automotive inventor believed that genius, including his own, resulted from long experience gained in the course of many previous lives.

The Best Way to Travel

There are many wrong ways to die — wrong in the sense that you remain stuck in the CYCLE OF BIRTH AND REBIRTH longer than need be. "Young" souls, in their first several incarnations, go through many short, brutal lifetimes in various physical bodies and spend many brief periods between resting unconsciously in lower spiritual dimensions because they haven't expanded their consciousness enough while in-body to realize that they are both human and divine. Each lifetime provides the opportunity for the human being to connect with their Spiritual Self, or Soul— to recognize that they are not merely a body, but a Soul wearing a temporary coat of skin in order to experience the physical world first hand. One cannot directly experience the physical world without a body. From this realization of your True Self and your spiritual nature comes the acceptance of the after-life as a spiritual being through knowing that your consciousness goes on after your physical body dies, in some less solid form, in some less dense dimension. *It's like putting away your winter coat when Spring comes, you know that the coat is shabby and you don't want to wear it anymore. That's virtually what death is all about.*[13]

Dying the right way is in full consciousness, knowing exactly where to go and what to do — before and after you leave your physical body behind to release your Soul to its highest spiritual potential. Once you know and incorporate the art of dying into your consciousness, you will be able to live your life more fully. You will be free of fear of death and this life will take on a deeper meaning for you. The ultimate moment of your life is your death! Make the most of it!

Walt Whitman

The great American poet believed in the essential divinity of humankind, and that we would eventually become gods, having already risen through the ranks of creation from rocks and trees.

The Tour Guide

It is time to take the mystery and the fear out of dying by creating a position for an earthly transitional guide and writing a book of instructions that people of today can relate to on how to die well . . .with joyful awareness!

The Ancient Egyptians called him Anubis, the god who led the dead to judgment. The Greeks gave the honor to Hermes and the Romans, to Mercury. In many religions and belief systems, there is the concept of an ETHERIC world angel, guide or intelligence whose function is to assist the dying person during their transition from the physical to the spiritual plane. The Japanese have a name for the act of making one's transition with ease and comfort, *anrakushi* [1], which is possible if one has been given the proper instructions, *anshi-jutsu* [1], prior to death. In Latin, the craft of dying without pain and suffering is called *ars moriendi* [1]. Eastern religions each had their own *Book of the Dead* [8, 25] containing instructions for departing earth life and journeying to the ETHERIC realms. Most of this information, however, was hoarded by their priests and lamas; kept secret from the general population who were not deemed worthy of receiving it nor capable of comprehending it. Native American tribes had *Shamans* who became channels, through their personal death-rite initiations, for healing as well as helping tribesmen make their transition to the ETHERIC world during their real death process. To Christians, Jesus is the SAVIOR who promised to lead them to Heaven. Contemporary religions use rituals performed by priests, rabbis or ministers to prepare the dying for their transition while the more secular-minded simply rely on the local funeral director to send them off.

Over time, the concept of life after death has been bandied about by theologians and scientists, scholars and students, priests and laypeople, TV talk show hosts and their guests, to no conclusion. It has not been a scientifically-provable thesis; therefore, it is left as a matter of faith. One either believes it or not. It seems that faith is necessary when we don't *know*. We may gather all the information and come to understand to a certain point, and then we have to make a leap of faith before we can accept something as fact. But when you have the experience, up close and personal, no leap of faith is required — you now *know* and you *know* you know. There is no question or doubt in your mind. Reverend Parrish-Hara wonders how many of those who say they believe in life after death have the courage of their convictions, or just hope? She calls this *the true test of facing death.*[20]

The only time one finds out for sure the true nature of reality is after death where the secret is safe from those who would abuse the knowledge. At least so thought the priests of ancient times. But times have changed and human beings have changed, and soon life after death will be proclaimed a scientific fact (by quantum physics) and instructions to prepare oneself for one's transition and life hereafter will become common knowledge. The majority of the lifewave of beings now on earth have evolved enough to truly comprehend the benefits of preparing for the transition to life after death as the precursor to living life on earth more peacefully — once they have the necessary information.

The real experience of life after death comes from those of us, especially children[17], who have died and come back to describe our experiences on the other side. In ages past, only the highest initiates of the temples or the initiated shamans, got to experience "near-death" and receive instructions for helping others make their transition easier. Now everyday people all over the world, millions of us, are being annointed as way-showers for those who are ready to achieve their highest developmental potential. The wonderful thing about having a near-death experience (NDE) is that you get another chance to change your life in the same lifetime; whereas final death requires a whole 'nother life-time to get it. Once you have experienced the overwhelming Love of God during an NDE, you cannot go back to the mundane world you lived in before, or, at least, not take it so seriously!

This guidebook will not mean anything to those who are not yet ready to receive their heritage as divine-human beings, but many more will pay enough attention to be able to get it right in their next life. Most important are those who are ready to prepare themselves now for the most significant event in their lives.

The reason I didn't "die" when I drowned in a white-water river accident 20 years ago was because I had a mission to accomplish on earth before I could remain permanently in spiritual realms. This I was told by a Being of Light as it showed me about spiritual life after death during my NDE. I was given the KEY TO LIFE and sent back to become a teacher helping others prepare for their transition and guide them through the process until they meet their ETHERIC guide on the other side.

Core NDErs are people who know, but they do not merely have a certain knowledge of matters . . . they have become what they know; their knowledge lives and grows within them. It is as if the core of the NDE becomes their core. The NDE is, then, not merely an experience that becomes a cherished memory that people may later take comfort in. It is not even just an experience that "changes one's life." It is one's life. And it becomes the source of one's true being in the world.

Unless this is understood about NDErs in general and core NDErs — that is, those that have experienced this spiritual radiance most deeply — in particular, what is most essential about them will not be grasped. And what they are capable of teaching the rest of us will then be lost.[22]

For lack of a modern term to describe a human being who functions as a guide on this side, I defer to *Anubis* and call us ANUBISISTS.

Orientation

This is not a secterian religious book nor does it require belief in an after-life to be useful to you. Its significance will become clear to you only when you die. It is based on the real experience of a human being who died and came back in order to let others know what they will experience during their death, which is actually the process of spiritual rebirth. This is not being written by one who adheres to any particular religious philosophy, but by one who has considered the thought of many doctrines and teachers and found there is some truth in every religion. The information in this guidebook may be used by any person of any faith, or of no faith — anytime during your transition when you realize the real illusion and remember something of the instructions.

There are a number of concepts used in this book that are little understood and open to various interpretations. These terms are capitalized throughout the book and defined in the appendix. Whether or not you are familiar with the concepts, you might want to read them over before going on to the next page to keep things in context, and then refer to them as needed later for clarification. These concepts are an integral part of the death-rebirth process and must be considered in order to begin to comprehend the experience before you die. What may not be clear to you now, will become very clear when you find yourself in the experience.

Giordano Bruno

This 16th Century Italian philosopher taught that a soul passed from one body to another and could ultimately attain perfection. He was burned at the stake as a heretic.

Plan Ahead

There are three important reasons for you to have knowledge of the death process beforehand, besides the obvious one that everyone, prepared or not, dies:

1. *Everyone is offered the opportunity for SALVATION, or Liberation from the CYCLE OF LIFE AND DEATH, at death;*

2. *This opportunity may be missed due to ignorance or fear of death and the unknown; and*

3. *The opportunity won't come again until after you incarnate and face death again.*[3]

You have a choice: This lifetime, or the next, or the next . . . Mastering the techniques of dying makes this death a certain opportunity for SALVATION or, at the very least, valuable time in the higher spiritual realms rather than an extended BARDO journey and rebirth relatively quickly.

Benjamin Franklin

Franklin was originally a printer by trade. He said that he looked forward to a second edition of himself, in which he hoped that the errata of the first edition might be corrected.

Womb With a View

The death-rebirth experience will vary from individual to individual in specific details although, generally, it is a similar experience, one of only two shared by *all* human beings. Just as the embryo passes through evolutionary development in the womb and emerges the product of its inherited genes and KARMA, consciousness goes through a similar evolutionary process during death. The physical body is the womb of consciousness. Death is the birth of the Soul from the womb of the body—like the butterfly emerging from its cocoon as it flexes its wings and flies away. The brain is the generative organ for the Soul at death. The Crown CHAKRA is the vagina which expands to allow the Soul rebirth into the spiritual body.[3] During this journey to rebirth, memories of its lifetime are relived and the Soul emerges with the attributes and KARMA it acquired during that life experience. Although the BARDO experience is determined by your KARMA, you still have Free Will. The choices you make will influence the end result. The more knowledge you have now, the better choices you will make then.

Victor Hugo

The French novelist wrote that when he died it would be as if he had merely finished a day's work -- which he would resume the next morning.

Road Maps

What determines the course of your death experience?

For one thing, how you die.

If death follows a long illness or extreme old age, you may have established contact with the other side during this time. You may have visited or been visited by deceased loved ones in full consciousness. You may have spent time preparing your spiritual *house, not made with hands, eternal in the heavens.* (2COR 5:1) You may have made plans for your future life in the spiritual domain. As your physical body has deteriorated, you have been building your beautiful spiritual form. When your physical body dies, you may simply move from the material to the spiritual world with full awareness.

If you die suddenly, unexpectedly in an accident, you may be thrown out of your body into a world you cannot comprehend and it may take sometime for you to realize what has happened and to accept that you are dead. If you have a heart attack or are electrocuted or drown or are murdered, or have an accident for which you are hospitalized for a time before you die, you may linger over your body for a while, watching the scene of your death from above, before letting go.

Dante Gabriela Rossetti

The English painter, poet and member of the pre-Raphaelite movement, which revived a medieval style of painting, was a believer in reincarnation. In his poem "Sudden Light: he wrote: "I have been here before . . . You have been mine before." He also wrote "A light there is in the beyond which makes the creator visible to the creature, who only in beholding him finds peace."

Are We There Yet?

If you suddenly find there has been a drastic change from one moment to the next, as could happen with sudden death, but you still feel alive though everything around you seems familiar but different, try to touch something — if your hand goes through it, you are dead — or having an NDE! Immediately call out the name of someone close to you who has already died... if you see them before you, you will know. Everything around you may seem the same — and it is, only that *you're experiencing it in a different way. That's the main difference between life and death. One of the problems...in between lives is familiarity and the apparent ordinariness of the situation.*[10]

When you notice you are observing your body from somewhere above your body, you realize that even though you are no longer part of that body, you can see and hear and are conscious of everything that is going on around it. You find that if you *think* about a loved one or about being some special place, you will suddenly be with that person or in that place. To your dismay, you find that people cannot hear you, do not even know you are present; that you are able to pass through solid walls; that the physical world no longer exists for you and you no longer exist for it. When you recognize that you are indeed dead, you may choose to say silent goodbyes to your loved ones — if it occurs to you that you may do so. If you are unable to accept that you have died or to let go of emotional ties to the physical world, you may wander aimlessly between two worlds; unable to get back into one, unwilling to go into the next.

<u>Robert Browning</u>

*The English poet and husband of Elizabeth
Barrett Browning wrote in his poem "Evelyn
Hope" that two lovers will be reunited after
one has died, though "delayed it may be for
more lives yet."*

Letting Go

What enables most to release their attachment to the material world fairly quickly is the overwhelming sense of peace and love which pervades one's consciousness upon leaving the body. There is no sense of loss. All pain and fear, sorrow and guilt fall away. If you had any handicaps or disabilities or disease, they disappear and you become "whole." You feel free and completely alive. All your senses are heightened and sharpened. You see all that you were blind to before.

> . . . when the perfect comes, the imperfect will pass away . . . now we see in a mirror dimly, but then face to face. Now I know in part; then I shall understand fully, even as I have been fully understood.
>
> 1COR 13:10,12

You feel drawn toward the love which manifests as a tiny brilliant light far in the distance. As you release your need to be back in your body, you find yourself rising higher and higher above the scene of your death— above the buildings, above the trees, above the earth, until you enter a black void. You feel yourself moving faster and faster as if reaching the speed of light, which gives you the sensation of speeding through a tunnel. Ahead you will see the Light, coming closer and closer.

Dame Edith Sitwell

The English poet often remarked on her striking resemblance to the Tudor English king Henry VII and his grand-daughter, Queen Elizabeth I. Dame Edith suggested that she may have been Henry VII in a former life.

Through the Tunnel

Going "through the tunnel" is the interpretation of a mind which has never shifted from one state of consciousness to another, as can be experienced during deep meditation. The gap in time is experienced as movement, but is actually a change in frequency domain, or the movement of awareness from one level to another. What is thought to be a tunnel is a transitional zone between states of consciousness.[21] The Light is the opening to the new state of consciousness and when one breaks through to that level, it appears as an explosion of White Light breaking into all its rainbow colors. Once the consciousness becomes adjusted to the new frequency or accustomed to the Light, you begin to perceive your experience in a new way.

<u>Origen</u>

"To the literal-minded we teach the Gospel in the historic way, preaching Jesus the Christ and him crucified. But to the proficient, fired with the love of divine wisdom, we impart the Logos (the Word)."

Finding Your Gate

You will have three opportunities to go to the Light and ascend to higher spiritual dimensions, but you will encounter experiences along the way which may distract you. Failure to reach the Light after the third opportunity will result in immediate rebirth into the physical world. However, before that happens, you may find yourself meeting deceased relatives, a guardian angel or other spiritual guides, who come to assist you in your transition. There will be workers on the otherside to help you get acclimated. You may find yourself in a strange, bewildering, but beautiful and somehow familiar environment in another dimension to which your guide has brought you for some learning purpose. You may find yourself in the Hall of the AKASHIC RECORDS absorbed in your life review. You may experience bizarre or frightening images that appear and disappear from view. Or you may find yourself in the middle of your worst nightmare having a *hellish* experience. The life you just left behind and your reactions during your BARDO journey will determine your entrance into the next.

A person who lives a spiritually unawakened lifetime, indulging only in the physical sensations and pleasures of the material world, expressing selfishness, hatred and lust, will not recognize the CLEAR LIGHT, will remain oblivious to the higher spiritual dimensions, and will probably choose to return quickly to the more familiar scene of their passion. The dying person who has failed during their life to attain any measure of spiritual awareness will think they are physically involved in a bizarre or frightening experience. This is what a young Soul goes through until, after many incarnations, it awakens to the spiritual world while still in a physical form. This unawakened Soul will go through many tumultuous after-death experiences (ADE) with no hope of any rest until it can get back to the physical world.

If you are one who expressed very little love in your physical lifetime, you cannot expect to be showered with it when you return to the spiritual world. Until you recognize the errors of your ways and demonstrate contrition, you will continue to have negative experiences. When you choose to repent, you may gain access to higher realms or you may choose to reincarnate quickly to compensate for the KARMA you accumulated in your previous life.

If you were a good person who was always nice to others and never did anything terribly wrong, but never woke up to your spiritual nature, you will have a pleasant transition followed by a long period in a peaceful state. As Plato taught, *the soul cannot fully come into human form if it has never seen the truth.*[5] Just living a "good" life and being a "nice" person isn't enough to lift you to spiritual heights when you die. Although you will not suffer any punishment, without the knowledge of the opportunity death offers, you will rest unconsciously in the spiritual realms as you lived your life on earth until you get restless and decide to reincarnate to get on with your spiritual progression.[3]

If you were a person who actively participated in life, did some good and some not so good things, but found God and through forgiveness became loving, caring and compassionate toward all life, you will move quickly from your life review into the Secondary Light and experience spiritual rewards. You may choose to reincarnate for a brief time for a special reason at various times, but your focus will be on further development in a spiritual dimension.

<u>Seneca</u>

"This life is only a prelude to eternity for that which we call death is but a pause, in truth a progress into life."

The Pearly Gates

The Souls of average persons alive today are partially awakened and their ADEs will be less fear-filled, depending on their level of awareness, than their previous ADEs. They will experience what they believe to be true at the time of their death. If it is pearly gates or streets paved with gold or happy hunting grounds, it will be so. If it is unconsciousness forever or until some expected event (e.g., Judgment Day), it will be so. The transition that takes place at death is in form only. Who you are is who you are. Once on the higher dimensions, the limitations of the mind constrained by the brain fall away and, when this is recognized, real spiritual progress begins. However, perceptions are limited by how limited your perceptions were while in body.

The THOUGHT-FORMS which dominate your deepest consciousness affect your spiritual form and experience. The power of thought becomes more evident to the awakened mind of the more advanced Soul when they realize in the spiritual dimensions that they have a great deal of mental power which they must quickly learn to control. Negative thoughts must be eliminated while in the physical form before a Soul is able to reach this state of consciousness. There are serious consequences in the form of destructive energies on the spiritual level if you don't forgive others and yourself while still in your body. The inability to forgive on earth will result in a limited spiritual existence and the desire to move higher will cause you to want to incarnate again to raise your consciousness during your next physical lifetime. You must descend again in order to ascend.

<u>Carl Jung</u>

The German psychoanalyst, who himself had a near-death experience, believed that "one's life is prolonged in time by passing through different bodily existences."

The Goal

The person who has awakened to their spiritual nature, expressed love throughout their daily life, and overcome the need for material things and physical pleasures, becomes the highly advanced Soul who will pass peacefully into the higher vibratory dimensions upon physical death without experiencing the turmoil of the lower dimensions. *"For the Christ-like being, the special meaning of a life consists, aside from abstention from serious moral transgressions, in positive deeds of selfless love that nourish the world."*[23]

If you reconnected with your spiritual nature while in your physical body and dedicated your life to doing God's work on earth, whether through knowledge, meditation or service, you may intuitively know to go straight to the CLEAR LIGHT at the moment of physical death. This foreknowledge enables one to achieve SALVATION, break the CYCLE OF BIRTH AND REBIRTH and become an individualized spirit taking their place as a fully-realized Child of God in the highest dimension. This is the goal every Soul aspires to achieve through one of its incarnations.

Immanuel Kant

The German philosopher believed that souls existed prior to earthly life and that they traveled to other planets after inhabiting human bodies.

Going Through Customs

You cannot cheat the system nor strike a bargain —
your vibrations will give your away. Knowing All cannot help you if you still have hatred, resentment or
darkness in your heart. You can only rise to the dimension or be attracted to the Light which closely matches
your own frequency. Love in your heart and living a life
filled with kindness and compassion raises your frequency rate. You can only tolerate being as close to the
Light as you have been open to the Light during your
physical lifetime. Your inner light or frequency must
match the frequency of the CLEAR LIGHT for you to
go into it. The CLEAR LIGHT is that which appears to
everyone just prior to the moment of death, but few
even see it.

Voltaire

The Italian philosopher affirmed reincarnation to be "neither absurd nor useless . . . It is no more surprising to be born twice than to be born once . . . everything in nature is resurrection."

It's a Jungle Out There

It is our choice to recognize that we are more than physical beings forced to survive in a hostile world. It is our purpose to understand that we are much more than our body, our emotions, our intellect and our ego. It is our quest to discover that we are highly evolved spiritual beings who projected a part of our consciousness into a physical form in the world of matter to learn more about existence in the physical dimension. It is our dilemma to experience physical sensations and pleasures without becoming attached to them. We need to become aware that we gave ourselves a limited amount of time in which to accomplish our mission after which we will return to our Soul, leaving our physical form behind, and that we must account for that lifetime.

Our Soul sends many aspects of ItSelf to experience many lifetimes on physical worlds in order to achieve its highest spiritual potential in the Kingdom of God. This means nothing to me, the incarnated human being, during my sojourn on earth. Our greatest concerns are a roof over our head, where our next meal is coming from, when we will find a job, whether we will find a mate. Our reality *is* the physical plane. The illusion is that *it* is *all* there is. The truth is that everything material decays over time. It is temporary. It is not real. We take none of it but the Love we expressed with us to the real world, the spiritual world, which is eternal. The solution lies in learning to enjoy living no matter what circumstances we are in at the moment.

Now isn't that a interesting challenge we set for ourselves! We have all this karmic stuff to deal with and we're supposed to enjoy it! The *key* is to recognize problems as karmic circumstances and to figure out what they are trying to teach us. When we "get it," the circumstances will change (though not necessarily for the better, much to our dismay, as there may be further lessons to be learned on our path to Self-discovery). Enter the KEY TO LIFE.

The pursuit of knowledge and wisdom should occupy our time — learning how to be *in* the physical world without becoming attached to its pleasures or caught up in its troubles. No matter what, it is only temporary. It will be over in a flash. If we become conscious of our reason for being while in a physical body, we retain what we learned after death and go on to higher planes of life. If not, our Soul will soon choose rebirth into the physical world to try again to reconnect while in body.

Déjà Vu

Each time we return, we arrive without a clue as to why we are here or what we are supposed to do. We conveniently "forget" our reason for coming during our transition to physical birth. Some just take longer than others to wake up! It's not that each human being isn't special or that one's lifetime isn't important. It is for human beings that the physical universe exists. That makes us very significant and implies our higher purpose for existence.

It is through our human experiences that we are eventually able to reunite with the Godhead as fully-developed, individualized Spiritual Beings. Each human lifetime is a step up the ladder toward Unity. Birth and rebirth are the process by which we progress toward Greater Self-Realization. Our dying to the physical world is simply a letting go of material things and physical limitations in order to express ourselves as we really are in our true spiritual home. At death, we remember why we came and our life review accounts for our successes and failures, our strengths and our weaknesses, according to our incoming goals.

At physical death, the illusion about what is real falls away and we see clearly the true reality of the spiritual dimensions. Death is *a transition from one state to another, or . . . an entry into a higher state of consciousness or of being.*[15] It was there all the time, but our limited physical senses kept it from us and convinced us that the physical world was all there was.

<u>Aristotle</u>

"Whatsoever be within us that feels, thinks, desires and animates is something celestial, divine . . . and consequently, imperishable."

On the Road Again

In the BARDO, we find *not unilateral judgment, but rather cooperative development towards the ultimate end of self-realization.*[15] It doesn't take long to remember that Love was the only thing that really mattered and to regret that we didn't know then what we know now. However, one of the worst things a dying person can do is to hold the thought of all their perceived "sins" in their mind as they are dying.[3] Repentance and forgiveness must be dealt with long before death occurs.[4] *Throughout life, the soul feels, at least faintly, that each time it passes a judgment on others that should rightly have been reserved for itself, it becomes a stranger to itself. Even the satisfaction of righteous anger and just punishment of others for their misdeeds is shallow and empty; they inevitably distort the true face of the soul.*[23] It is by learning these things now, while still in a physical form that our death becomes an integral part of our life cycle and may be looked forward to with great anticipation and renewed respect.

None of this is intended to imply that death is to be rushed into frivolously, for there is KARMA to be considered in suicide, such as the selfishness of it, the lack of consideration by abandoning others, and for attempting to interrupt cosmic timing; compensation will have to be extracted in subsequent lifetimes.

Your experience following physical death will depend upon the way you lived your life — your intentions, the motives behind your behaviors, the love you expressed, how you treated others, whether you came to know God and to recognize who you truly are. You will be the judge of your lower consciousness actions. As many NDErs report, judgment comes from within themselves, not from any outside source.[15] No one is more critical than your Soul and no one is more loving and patient and willing to give you another lifetime to do better. The more love you express in your daily life, the more pleasant will be your death experience and subsequent lifetimes.

To Plan Or Not To Plan

You can choose to use this information, whether or not you believe in life after death, or you can choose to take your chances. In the case of the latter, you are likely to experience a *breech* [9] death and spend more time than you want in lower spiritual dimensions and reincarnate with appropriate disabilities. It is important to *KNOW WHAT IS GOING ON* at your death, no matter how or when you die. Without the knowledge, you will be faced with your greatest fears at the time when you should be free of fear. Even if the stages leading up to your death are painful or terrifying, the moment of death, especially when you have properly prepared yourself in advance, is an incredibly wonderful, mind-boggling experience.

With all of this in mind, the following guidebook will describe the physical death-spiritual rebirth experience for those who are ready to receive this teaching.

> . . . the interior view of death does not deny or seek to romanticize the process of dying. That, of course, is often painful, both for the dying person and those near. And near-death experiencers rarely say they lose their fear of dying; it is only of death itself that fear is dissolved . . . It is in that moment — from the standpoint of inner experience — that, metaphorically, the grim reaper is transmuted into the being of light, and pain gives way to inner peace. [22]

Johann Wolfgang von Goethe

The German writer and artist was certain "that I have been here, as I am now, a thousand times before, and I hope to return a thousand times."

Things to Do Before You Go

If you are a highly advanced Soul (one who has experienced numerous lifetimes and reconnected with your Divine Self along the way), who desires to make this lifetime your last necessary incarnation, you will want to begin training for your final journey now, even if you expect to live many more years in your present body. The sooner you plan to embark upon your death-rebirth journey, the more intense must be your practice, especially if you have not done so until now. Even if you are only a beginner on your spiritual path and have chosen to get the most spiritual opportunity you can out of this life, knowing you probably have too much KARMA to overcome and will have to reincarnate for at least one more physical lifetime, you will do your Soul immense good by practicing to the best of your ability for the remainder of this one.

In order to be able to recognize the CLEAR LIGHT at the moment of death and hold on to it, —

1. Learn to meditate to the point of being able to shut out all distractions and maintain your attention on seeing the CLEAR LIGHT. The practice of KUNDALINI meditation, no matter what level you attain, will activate this spiritual energy, which has the potential to transmute your sexual energy into creativity and bring about illumination (a vision of the CLEAR LIGHT). You may not get to see it in this life, but it may help you considerably during your death journey.

If you have become dependent on prescription drugs, meditation practice may also help you manage chronic pain and the pain of terminal illness. Medications should be continued while you are learning, but, in many cases and under the direction of your physician, you may be able to lower your dosages and overcome your dependency. Most people find it easier to take a pill than to take the time to learn to meditate efficiently; yet, if you do, you will find you are in control of your pain and not controlled by your pain.

2. Spend some time each day connecting with your spiritual self, your Soul. Attain a deep devotion and reverence toward the SAVIOR or Master you love most. That connection established before death will aid you greatly during your journey. This devotion will stir up the gift of God within (sometimes before death, often at death) and open you to SALVATION.

3. Attempt to dissolve all the karmic bonds you have accumulated in this lifetime and to uncover the unknown KARMA carried over from previous lives in order to right all your wrongs. Seek forgiveness from those whom you have hurt and forgive those who have wronged you— no matter how difficult it is for you to do that. Pay back your debts and forgive those debts owed to you. Replace any monstrous THOUGHT-FORMS you have created by thinking the most extraordinarily beautiful thoughts you can to overcome them — otherwise you will get to meet some ugly stuff in

the shadows of the BARDO — guaranteed! Replace violence with understanding, greed with giving, hate with compassion, guilt with forgiveness, lust with creativity. Overcome evil with good to the best of your ability.

4. Prepare yourself mentally and emotionally to die in full consciousness, anticipating merging with the CLEAR LIGHT. If you are drugged, no matter how prepared you are otherwise, you may miss it because it comes in a flash <u>before</u> you die.

5. Avoid accumulating any more karmic attachments. Recognize that you are building your ASTRAL form and spiritual home out of your thoughts and emotions, as recorded in your Heart SEED ATOM. Giving into temptations of wrongdoing is unpleasant material you will have to deal with during your BARDO journey. Knowing to expect the CLEAR LIGHT and what you will have to go through if you miss it, or the Secondary Light, because of your karmic baggage will help you subconsciously avoid karmic-producing choices.

There are many books and classes and teachers and techniques available today, but you must learn to discern, to trust your intuition, to find those which are "right" for you. To integrate these practices into your life will take more than reading a single book or attending a single class or practicing a single technique, and takes more time than you might think. You must be diligent and persistent in your pursuit of right knowledge. The more you come to know, the more questions you will have. Never stop learning — all of your life is school, including your dying experience. In discerning truth from falsity, you must learn to tune-in to your inner spiritual guide. Do not fall victim to those who tell you they know the right way for you or who use flattery or other subtle manipulation to get you to follow them. Pay attention to your gut feeling and check the facts — keep asking questions. Keep the focus of your life on your spiritual future and enjoy this life to the fullest in the meantime.

Preparing For D-Day

This process (Reincarnation) is not interrupted by death. Change continues in the constituents of the organism other than the gross body which has been cast off and which undergoes changes of its own. But there is a difference: the after-death change is merely the result of the action of accumulated past Karma and does not, as in earthly life, create new Karma, for which a physical body is necessary. There is no breach of consciousness, but a continuity of transformation. Death consciousness is the starting point, followed by the other states of consciousness . . .[25]

While some people enjoy the spontaneity of taking off on a trip with no map and no itinerary, most people prefer to do some amount of preplanning for a journey — and this most important journey of your life is no exception. It's not that you won't get through it without planning — you've probably done it hundreds of times already—but that the goal of the Soul is freedom from the CYCLE OF LIFE AND DEATH; and, until you are able to recognize the CLEAR LIGHT when it first dawns and hold onto it at one of your deaths, you keep yourself tied to the earth. To gain that freedom, you must be able to die in full consciousness, with your mind wide open to the Light of God. If you want more than just a glimpse of this overwhelming Light and ecstatic feeling of God's Love, if you want to be able to hold onto that experience and merge with it to experience Oneness with God for the rest of eternity, then you must have enough Love in your Heart SEED ATOM to vibrate at the same frequency as the CLEAR LIGHT by the time of your death.

You may not be ready to let go of the need for the pleasures and sensations of physical life at the end of your present life and prefer to be able to come back as soon as possible to enjoy it further. And that's O.K. Take as many lives as you like. But keep this book around — you may feel the urge to read it again some day, perhaps in some other lifetime!

Those who have recognized the Light in <u>this</u> life and feel ready to progress further in the next world have already started the process of dissolving their KARMA and preparing themselves, by raising their vibrational frequency, to recognize the CLEAR LIGHT at the end of this lifetime. Some of these will still need to come back again for karmic reasons or want to come back to visit for a while for higher reasons, and others are ready to develop their greater potential on higher planes.

Most people fall somewhere in between and aren't sure what they believe. But many will, at the urging of their inner voice, realize they might as well prepare themselves somewhat, just in case it is true! As someone once said, *Why not believe in God or accept Christ in your life? If it turns out to be true, it'll be a good thing. If it turns out not to be true, it certainly won't do you any harm.* The value of preplanning will hit them when they die and they'll remember something about what to expect.

With terminal illness or old age, there is time before you are confined to bed:

- to right wrongs
- to practice forgiveness
- to release your attachments to material things and physical pleasures

- to re-establish your connection to your God-Self (whatever that means to you)

- to prepare yourself with relaxation and meditation exercises and practice raising your KUNDALINI energy in order to die in full consciousness so you will recognize the CLEAR LIGHT when it dawns

- to write your final instructions in your own words and practice with a Reader or ANUBISIST, who will guide you through your dying experience by keeping you on track

- to prepare your death room, according to your beliefs, and desires. As Dr. Kubler-Ross says, *Dying is hard under any circumstances, but dying in the familiar surroundings of one's home, with those you love and who love you, can take away much of the fear.*[12]

We will each have our own spiritual karmic path to travel, which we designed by the way we conducted the physical life-opportunity we are leaving behind. While there are many similarities during the early stages of the physical death-spiritual rebirth experience, each of us is the author of our own book and most of what we experience after death will be a very, very personal experience; indeed, adventure!

If your death is sudden or unexpected, as in an accident or a heart attack, you can still be prepared (at least for your death experience itself; compassion, forgiveness and spiritual enlightenment must be practiced daily throughout your life to be fully prepared to die, unexpectedly) if you have read this book, written your instructions and arranged to have them read upon news of your death. You will have prepared yourself in that you will know what is happening, recall your instructions and tune-in to your Reader without delay.

In the case of sudden death, you will leave your body before impact and view the scene of it's demise from a point above the scene. The quicker you turn your attention away from the physical world and your physical form, by recognizing that you are dead and immediately need to *know* what is happening to you, the better will be your opportunity to merge with the CLEAR LIGHT when it first dawns, or the Secondary light as soon as it appears. If you have practiced with a Reader, you will be able to tune-in to the Reader's voice (frequency) no matter how far apart the two of you are. Previous contact with a guide (SAVIOR, angel, teacher or loved one) on the other side will assure you won't stay long in this stage through ignorance and confusion. Wandering around the spiritual world without a map or a plan will lose you many opportunities for spiritual growth.

As to whether a person should be told death is imminent in the case of a medical diagnosis, that is of course up to the individuals involved; however, depriving a person of the opportunity to take full advantage of their dying experience is not going to benefit this person and, in all likelihood, will hinder their transition because they may feel resentment or bitterness after death at not being told. The last thoughts at death are important to the departing Soul. Our last earth memory should be of the joyful faces of our loved ones. If you can't bring yourself to tell the person, find someone who can. Many people learn the truth anyway, especially near the end when they begin experiencing consciousness shifts in the early stages of their death process. It would be so much better for the dying person to know what to expect than be frightened by it. A conspiracy of silence should not be built around a dying person. This is a time when compassion, truthfulness, trust and love should be expressed so dying persons will not feel lonely and abandoned at this important time in their lives.

Two hospice nurses, Maggie Callanan and Patricia Kelley, wrote a wonderful book called *Final Gifts*[2] describing what they learned about the dying experience from their patients' messages as they drifted in and out of awareness of this life and the next. They have called the period preceding death from old age or terminal illness *Nearing Death Awareness* and describe what the dying person and their loved ones go through during the last months, weeks, days, hours and minutes before the heart stops beating. They compare Nearing Death Awareness similarly to a Near-Death Experience except that the NDE is usually sudden while the former occurs gradually over time.

Again, knowing what to expect and what needs to be done gives everyone involved greater peace of mind. Trying to understand what the dying person is trying to communicate instead of drugging them or brushing off their attempts to communicate allows them a more peaceful death. Callanan and Kelley[2] point out the importance of "reconciliation" before a peaceful death may come. There is often a need for completion, to settle things, to make things right, to finish some business. They observed that people seem to prolong their dying until there is closure or healing and often suffer intense emotional and spiritual pain until it is resolved. Sometimes the healing is needed between the dying person and other people, sometimes it is something within themselves (guilt, shame, regrets, hatred, anger), and sometimes it is between them and their belief system.

All this is a prelude to the life review experienced in the BARDO journey. If reconciliation and forgiveness can be accomplished before death, it won't need to be experienced later. If the family around the dying person is aware they are Nearing Death Awareness and listen for the clues (because they are not usually direct), they can help the person overcome the obstacles to a peaceful dying experience. Callanan and Kelley suggest . . . *When someone you love is dying, you may not see the gifts, but only grief, pain and loss. However, a dying person offers enlightening information and comfort, and in return those close at hand can help bring that person peace and recognition of life's meaning.*[2]

What to Pack

The following are offered as guidelines for preparation. These are only suggestions to start you thinking about which preparations you want to make for your journey. They may be adapted to meet your religious beliefs, cultural traditions or your lifestyle.

OBTAINING A READER

The importance of having a Reader cannot be expressed strongly enough. No matter how spiritual you are or how prepared you think you are, finding yourself in another dimension is such an awesome change that you can be easily distracted by the wonder of it all.

Without a Reader to constantly remind you to go to the Light, you might be tempted to hang around your body, your home or your loved ones until opportunities have been lost.

Without a Reader to constantly remind you that the images you are experiencing are merely mental reflections of your predominant thoughts in life and cannot (physically) harm you, you may linger in a frightening dimension longer than need be.

Without a Reader to remind you to call out to your SAVIOR, you may not remember that help is at hand; to let go of the material world and physical desires; and to repent and forgive, you may not get to experience the higher dimensions before you must incarnate again.

This is the one journey on which you do not want to carry any excess baggage, especially emotional baggage, and working with an ANUBISIST will help clear you for a smooth take-off into the spiritual dimension.

If you are a highly evolved spiritual seeker, you may not need a Reader, but you may want one just to be sure you stay on track. It is likely that you will merge directly with the CLEAR LIGHT and may only want the first part of the instructions read. Most people, however, will need the Reader to continue for three or more days after death with Part III, and only the most depraved person will require the last section to be read for quite some time.

As to whom to chose as a Reader, a close friend or family member would be ideal — if they can keep their emotions in check. Their crying and lamenting will only be another distraction for you, keeping you from merging with the Light. You might want to read you own instructions into a tape recorder, although even hearing your own voice might distract you from your course (the habit of attraction), and arrange for someone you trust to play the tape according to your instructions. A minister or priest may come to your bedside and administer any last rites you deem necessary, but they then leave. They do not sit at your bedside until you die or read over your body for hours and continue, if it is necessary, to read for you for days or months afterward. Therefore, you may want to make arrangements with an ANUBISIST. This professional will help you write your personalized instructions, practice with you beforehand, be on call when your death becomes imminent and at your side when you depart or begin reading for you (to a prepared effigy) as soon as news of your sudden death arrives; and continue reading for you, intuitively, as long as necessary. With prearrangement, you will be tuned-in to his or her voice and easily follow that guidance until you meet your spiritual guide on the other side who will take you the rest of the way.

THE ROOM

If you know your death is imminent, you will likely want to arrange to die in your own home, surrounded by your loved ones, but this isn't always possible. If you are hospitalized, you may still be able to arrange for some of the following suggestions if the hospital staff is amenable.

Orange Light

The orange light stimulates the head centers. As KUNDALINI rises, it will exit the body with the lifeforce at the CHAKRA most habitually expressed during life, but it will be attracted to orange light and it is possible that the person may experience spiritual illumination for the first time if their energy can reach the head centers — even if only for a moment. This will provide a great spiritual boost for the dying person.[3]

Room Arrangements

Whenever possible, the dying person should be placed facing east. If candles and incense (preferably Sandlewood) are desired and not prohibited (as they might be in a hospital), they may be placed in the room. As for music, it is up to you, but it may be a distraction during transition. Mantrums or chanting, soothing classical or New Age music may be desirable in the earlier stages leading up to death, but it may be better for the dying person if it is turned off or down very low as symptoms advance. Doors and windows may be closed to maintain silence, especially if in a noisy environment.

Personal Objects

You may want to arrange or, if bed-ridden, have a care-giver arrange to have things meaningful to you placed around your bedside — family pictures, personal objects, flowers, religious symbols.

Preparing an Effigy

In case your death occurs away from home, you may want to arrange a table with a picture of yourself and several personal objects to be used in place of your body for the Reader to focus on.

RELATIVES

You may want to have your loved ones around you while you are making your transition, but they should be advised of your arrangements and your desire to die in full consciousness. It would be most helpful to you if those who are likely to have an outburst of emotion upon your death or if a family argument is likely to break out, that they be asked to leave the room and express themselves outside where you will not be distracted from your journey.

As to a person's decision about being present at the side of a dying loved one, no one can understand the true spiritual experience of the death journey until he or she experiences it him or herself. And regardless of your personal beliefs, it will be to the dying person's benefit if you are there for them at this time. Read *Final Gifts* [2] to find out what to expect as your loved one approaches death so you can be of help to them.

Relatives attending should be asked to direct their mental energies toward helping the dying person recognize the Light and move into it — either by joining with the Reader or repeating religious prayers or biblical passages you preselected; however, noise should be kept to a minimum so the departing consciousness can hear the Reader and listen for the Sound of Silence.

<u>Gen. George S. Patton Jr.</u>

The most foreceful commander of the second World War believed that he had been a Greek warrior who fought Cyrus the Persian. He also thought he had been a follower of Alexander the Great, and that he was present at the Battle of Crecy in 1346, during the Hundred Years' War between France and England.

What to Expect

FROM THE READER

The place for the Reader is at your side, near your head, so you can hear the early instructions clearly. The Reader will watch for the signs of approaching death and keep you aware that the CLEAR LIGHT will be dawning shortly. Signs for the Reader to watch for are:

> sagging facial muscles,
>
> labored breathing,
>
> glazed eyes,
>
> blueness beneath the fingernails,
>
> extreme coldness in the feet which gradually creeps upward.[3]

The dying person should be roused if he or she drifts off to sleep until breathing ceases to assure that the person will die in full consciousness. When the Reader begins, others in the room should concentrate on helping the dying person recognize the CLEAR LIGHT the moment the breath ceases. The person may be turned on his or her right side and the arteries in the throat may be pressed to keep them conscious as long as possible. When pain ceases and consciousness begins to expand, the Emotional SEED ATOM has departed the body. To those in attendence, it may appear the person has entered a coma, however they are not unconscious. Rather the consciousness has expanded to include the unseen fourth dimension. It is at this moment of expansion that the CLEAR LIGHT dawns and the heart beat ceases. The heart will still be beating as the CLEAR LIGHT dawns and the words of the Reader will help them hold to the Light as they leave their physical body. Coldness around the heart signifies cessation of the heartbeat, departure of the Heart SEED ATOM and, in most cases, the breaking of the SILVER CORD.[3] Reading should begin in the early stages to direct the dying person's attention to recognizing the CLEAR LIGHT and move on to Part II when the heart stops beating. The Reader should maintain calmness, serenity and detached concern, and gently urge the consciousness toward its spiritual rebirth. Read as if you were reading it to your self.

SIGNS AND SOUNDS OF DEATH

As death approaches, your Emotional SEED ATOM begins to loosen, any pain you have been experiencing disappears and you find yourself letting go of the physical world (the room you are in, the loved ones around you) and becoming more involved with the wonder of your dying experience. Though your awareness shifts back and forth, you continue to "hear" what goes on around your body, and even after you cross over.

The first sensation called by the Tibetans[25] "earth sinking into water" will be of becoming smaller and smaller — a mental experience of shrinking into the depths of a dark void. At the same time, you will lose control of your body's muscle tension and feel youself sinking into the bed. You will experience difficulty swallowing and not want food or water. You will appear to relax and become peaceful to observers. At any time, you may begin to hear snapping or popping noises. These are the sounds of the ETHERIC threads of your SILVER CORD breaking.

The next stage, the Tibetans call "water sinking into fire." You will feel alternating sensations of cold and heat. You may experience chills, chattering teeth and shivering followed by extreme irritability or agitation. These are the effects of KUNDALINI energy rising up the spinal column. If you have prepared yourself for this moment, you will be working with the energy to direct it to the Crown CHAKRA; if not, it may be frightening or, at least, uncomfortable.

The next sensation, the Tibetans call "fire sinking into air," will feel as if you are expanding and about to explode. Your breathing may become very labored. You may be hearing buzzing noises, high-pitched whistling, low rolling thunder. You may feel a band of pressure around your head as if your mind is about to blow. Your feet and hands may feel tingly, as if they have gone to sleep. Your body may feel fluid, like melting wax. You will begin to experience hallucinations, distorted images that rise and fade away. Lastly, you feel a vibration starting at your Root CHAKRA, rising upward along the spinal column, reaching toward your head. Then, suddenly, you burst into full consciousness at your last breath as the CLEAR LIGHT dawns. The CLEAR LIGHT is the reflection of your consciousness without any limitations or darkness. You will probably smile and may even sit up in bed and try to tell those in attendence that you have just seen God or your SAVIOR or Heaven or deceased realtives. And then your body will fall back onto the bed, your heart will stop beating and your wondrous rebirth journey into the spiritual world will commence . . . according to your KARMA.In this state between life and death, there is no space or time, no emotions or actions. There is only

Being in Bliss. To remain at One with the Light is to receive SALVATION. Merging with the Light does not mean annihilation. It does mean surrendering control of who you thought you were to become your Real Self. If you find yourself resisting or fear creeping in, relax and let go to the Light.

Death is itself only an initiation into another form of life than that of which it is the ending.[25]

The Journey's End

If your desire to again be in body and return to earth still dominates your consciousness, you are likely to seek immediate rebirth and forfeit any time on higher spiritual planes. Following your BARDO journey, you enter a trance state to prepare for your REINCARNATION process (deciding how to play out your KARMA in another physical body). This desire arises in those who spent their lives immersed in the lower impulses of earth life and want to return to their old habits — even though they subconsciously realize they will inherit a life filled with the same conditions they inflicted on others. They may even choose a form which reflects that torment to ease their previous karmic debts, and suffering may be the only way for them to evolve spiritually. Evil is a deliberate move away from God, with full awareness of selfish intent and no thought of repentence or spiritual progression. Suffering is merely the result of necessary purification, not punishment — made necessary by one's selfish actions, habits and thoughts.

Those Souls who move on to higher spiritual dimensions, those who raised their consciousness or frequency to the rate of the Secondary CLEAR LIGHT and were able to merge with it, will feel enfolded by a great silence, a peaceful ocean of light. As their superconscious awareness opens, they may be inclined to break into laughter at their blindness and dumbness of even thinking that earth life was reality when, here, just beyond the confines of the brain and body is the True Reality. All the teaching and training that they took for granted or did half-heartedly on earth now becomes most important and they will wish they had done more while still in body. If they tuned-in to their Reader, hopefully, they remembered that the reflections they saw in the BARDO were their own thoughts and memories and were able to pass through them quickly. Once through the BARDO, they will find themselves clothed in their ASTRAL bodies and guided by loved ones and spiritual guides to their new homes and lives that match their level of spiritual awareness. Their ASTRAL bodies will be either beautiful or have defects (not in the same sense as physical handicaps), depending on the quality of their thoughts during their earth lives and during their BARDO experiences. A person may have had a good Soul, but practiced some unwise habits during earth life. Their ASTRAL form will reflect these defects and they may be temporarily detained on a lower ASTRAL plane until they are purged — which is why it is better to overcome bad habits (e.g., smoking, drinking, drugs) while in body. You will ascend as rapidly as you overcome and rise as high as your inner light will allow you.

For those who arrive bewildered, there are guides to convince those who don't believe they are dead. They will take these Souls to visit their dead friends and relatives and even take them back to their earth homes to see those who are mourning their deaths or to the scene of their demise and show them that no one can see or hear them. They will lead them past incredible landscapes, beautiful cities of light with magnificent gleaming buildings[15] and show them their spiritual homes where everything they loved and lost is waiting for them. There they will be reunited with the ones they loved most while on earth. Their early experiences will reflect their beliefs about the after-life while on earth (e.g., streets of gold, happy hunting grounds, etc.), but they will gradually discover that it is more than they ever dreamed possible.

One of the things you will notice about the spiritual dimensions is that you still have the same senses you had before only they are a thousand times keener — not only that, but you will find you now have higher senses than even the psychic senses you may have developed while in your last body. With practice, you will be able to think things into being — the more you learned about the physical world, the better you will be able to recreate them in the spiritual dimension. It is merely rearranging atoms by mind force. You will be able to communicate telepathically with others and zip around your universe via instant thought-wave transportation. As you grow accustomed to your new life and let go of your false beliefs, you may find yourself seeking higher dimensions of God's universe, but you can only rise as high as the rate your vibration allows. If you want to ascend further, you will have to descend again into matter and will begin to prepare yourself for REINCARNATION in a physical form according to your remaining KARMA.

The highly-evolved Soul, who was able to merge with the CLEAR LIGHT at death, does not experience another BARDO journey or spend any time on the lower planes. As you melt into the CLEAR LIGHT, you become aware that you still have a body but you are Total Consciousness. As the crystallized structures of the earth dissolve away, your consciousness absorbs the inpouring of Divine Wisdom — Christ Consciousness. You will become aware of Light Beings all around you and of one special guide whose voice soothes your fears and guides you to higher planes. As you soar to blissful regions of light, you will hear glorious music. Out of the mist will emerge one solitary figure — the great Master or SAVIOR to whom you prayed and meditated while on earth. This day you are with them in "paradise" and have achieved SALVATION from the CYCLE OF LIFE, DEATH AND REBIRTH.[3] Of your life on the higher planes, not much can be told because our language is inadequate to describe spiritual existence. What could be described is more wondrous and meaningful than mere words can convey. But you will be involved with your higher spiritual development, existing in a refined spiritual body, living in glorious surroundings (similar to earth's, but less dense), still going to school and learning about "life", and, occasionally, returning to earth in a human body as a teacher to raise the consciousness of Humanity.

The Countdown

SCHEDULE

If the dying person is being monitored and the approach of death becomes evident, the Reader should be called to the bedside as final preparations are being made. If death occurs without warning, the Reader should be notified immediately and begin reading as soon as possible. The Reader should try to stay with the body for forty minutes to an hour after death; two hours, if possible, and reading should continue even if the body has to be removed.

If possible the reading of Part I should begin just prior to death and for twenty minutes after breathing stops as the Soul withdraws from the body. Part II follows for another twenty minutes as the Soul becomes aware it has left the body, and Part III continues for another hour after as the Soul moves into its BARDO journey. If it is considered necessary, Part IV may follow for the next hour and then be read twice daily for a predetermined time span.

Those in the room with a dying person, when they become aware that death is imminent, must remain absolutely quiet so the dying person may hear the Sound of the CLEAR LIGHT. Crying and wailing are distractions during the death experience. Silent whispers of encouragement to let go to the Light are most helpful. During this first phase of the BARDO, it is time to think of the departing Soul, not of your loss. It is best you leave the room if you cannot control your emotions. During the first few minutes following cessation of breathing, the person may temporarily regain consciousness and describe visions and deceased relatives. This may last up to half an hour. Relatives at the bedside should be loving and supportive, not doubting or patronizing.

DRUGS

While the dying person may be experiencing pain leading up to the moment death, just prior to death, all pain will cease as the Emotional SEED ATOM withdraws; therefore, drugs which block consciousness should not be administered in the last moments so the person may try to go consciously into the Light. There are two drugs available which will block pain but not affect consciousness: *Zeneperin* and the *Brompton* cocktail[3] and one should discuss them with their physician.

If consciousness blocking drugs or gas are used, the person will miss the CLEAR LIGHT and awaken to the Secondary Light. In this case, the Reader will help the Soul understand what has happened.

Departure Time

The first phase of the journey begins for the dying person before breath ceases and continues about twenty minutes after for the average person — with little-to-some spiritual awareness. It will be over in a flash for the highly evolved spiritual mind, and last much longer than twenty minutes for those who are spiritually unconscious — with little-to-no belief in God — at the time of their deaths.

If the dying person is using relaxation exercises and mediation prior to death, the Reader may encourage them according to prearrangements. If the person is working with KUNDALINI energy, the Reader may assist and, watching for physical signs of the rising energy, encourage him or her toward spiritual illumination at the same moment that the CLEAR LIGHT dawns. These activities are specialties of an ANUBISIST.

As the time of death approaches, begin to repeat the signals of the approaching CLEAR LIGHT to keep the person focused and remind them that the sensations they are experiencing are normal and there is nothing to fear. Those who have achieved acceptance of their death are likely to be more peaceful at this stage. The voice of the Reader is a gentle guide in the background. Listen to what the dying person is able to tell you about what they are experiencing and be supportive. They are not confused — they are amazed! Allow the dying person periods of silence (between read paragraphs) so they can go with the experience as their consciousness shifts back and forth. Try to read to them and express love to them when they are lucid in the physical world. Use your mental energy to direct them to the Light when they appear to go unconscious.

These stages and sensations are documented in many of the books in my bibliography.

Earth sinking into water —
you may be feeling pressure around you, that you are shrinking and falling inward.

Water sinking into fire —
you may experience being very cold and then very hot.

Fire sinking into air —
you may feel as if you are expanding upward and outward;
you may feel pressure around your head as your consciousness prepares to expand;
you may be feeling tingling sensations in your hands and feet;
your body may be feeling fluid, as if you are melting into the bed;
you may be experiencing the spiritual energy vibrations rising in your body towards your head.

Concentrate on the rising energy, move it up to the inner chambers of your brain and allow your consciousness to expand to meet the CLEAR LIGHT when it dawns.[3]

The dying person experiences momentary blackouts as consciousness is suspended during the transition of the Soul from one frequency to another in order to adjust to the new frequency, which is why this section is repeated several times. The experience in consciousness is to appear to jump from one state to another without memory of a passage. As many NDErs report, they *suddenly* find themselves above their bodies looking down at their bodies or they are suddenly whisked away to another place.[19] Some of these shifts may take place before breathing ceases and the dying person may suddenly sit up and indicate something about what they are experiencing. When such signals appear, it is time to begin reading Part I, calling their attention to the approaching CLEAR LIGHT. The actual death "moment" covers the first six minutes of death, therefore reading should be continuous. Always address the Soul of the dying person to whom you are reading. The following are examples of the kinds of words that are appropriate and may be adapted to your personal values and beliefs.

Salvador Dali

*The surrealist painter considered himself to
be a reincarnation of St. John of the Cross,
the 16th Century Spanish mystic of the
Carmelite Order.*

The Traveler's Guide[3, 6, 23]

PART I

Dear Soul of (name), the time has now come for you to see the True Reality. Your breathing is about to cease. You are coming face-to-face with the CLEAR LIGHT and true recognition of your Oneness with God.

At this moment, know thyself to be a perfect Child of God and become One with All That Is.

Keep your mind open and alert, concentrate on God and merging with the CLEAR LIGHT, know that you are loved and that you are Love.

Dear Soul of (name), let not your mind be distracted by thoughts of loved ones or material things left behind. Resolve to take advantage of this dying experience through love and compassion to merge with the CLEAR LIGHT and perfect your Soul.

Dear Soul of (name), allow the earth to fall away and become One with Light. Let go of the body that has been your home and become who you really are. Slip out of your skin and into your spiritual gown.

Let go and go to the Light. You will not lose yourself, you will find your True Self.

Dear Soul of (name), keep your attention on the Light and ignore anything else around you or thoughts that come to you.

*Listen for the Sound of the CLEAR LIGHT,
the heavenly clear flute sounds from your Source.*

*You have prepared yourself for this moment,
you know what to do.*

*Stay with the Light. Raise the light of your
inner consciousness to meet the CLEAR LIGHT of
God and hold onto the Light.*

*Let go and let God. Let go and become One
with God.*

*Dear Soul of (name), be not awed by the feeling
of overwhelming Love of God but become that
Love, for that is what you are.*

*Do not contract, but expand your consciousness
and merge with the Light.*

Become One with the Light.

*You are not separate from the Light, you are
the Light.*

*You are being reborn into the Light of Pure
Consciousness.*

For the highly evolved spiritual person, this reading will be sufficient and personal prayers may be used to close the deathbed ceremony.

If the person missed the CLEAR LIGHT or wasn't able to hold onto that transcendental state long enough to merge with it, they will awaken to experience the Secondary Light; for these Souls, Part II of the reading should commence 20 minutes after breathing has ceased.

PART II

Dear Soul of (name), concentrate on finding your SAVIOR (name, if known). Call out the name of the one who has your greatest devotion and Love.

Keep your attention on the Light and become one with it.

Know that you have departed from your physical body and that you are not, nor never were, your body.

You are and always have been a spiritual being, a perfect Child of God, a vibration of light.

Be not distracted.
Be not in awe.
Go to the Light.

You are not alone.
Concentrate on your symbol of Diety.
Call out to your SAVIOR.
See it with your whole being.

Become the Light.
Immerse yourself in the ocean of Love.
Assimilate the overwhelming Love which flows within and without.
Surrender your consciousness to the Light.

Dear Soul of (name), your initial bewilderment at what you are experiencing will quickly turn to astonishment because everything is so real,
so natural,
so perfect.

You may find it difficult to believe that you are dead because you feel very much alive.

You may wonder if you are dreaming, but you are not.

You may try to communicate with your loved ones left on earth, but they cannot hear you.

It is time to let go of the physical world and turn your attention to finding the Light.

Be not distracted by the visions around you. Remember that they are only reflections of your lower consciousness and cannot harm you.

Turn and face your fears and delusions, but do not dwell on them.

Seek the Light that shines for you and call on your SAVIOR to guide you on your journey.

Repeat Part II for about twenty minutes while directing your mental energy to helping the departed Soul merge with the Secondary Light.

If the Traveler is unable to hold onto the Light, another opportunity will arise for them in the state of karmic apparitions. Here their crystallized THOUGHT-FORMS begin to appear and disappear, from heavenly visions to the darkness of their evil thoughts.

During this phase, they will also view their former physical body being taken away and whatever is done to it following their death. They will see their loved ones' reactions to their death and hear them calling to them. They may experience a longing to return to their physical body, though most will close off from the physical world after they realize no one can see or hear them.

The Reader will encourage them to turn away from the physical world and seek the Light by reading Part III for an hour.

PART III

Dear Soul of (name), listen to my voice with full attention.

Be not distracted by the ethereal sounds,
the brilliant lights,
the beautiful rays of color.

Be not in awe of what you see.

Be not frightened by what appears to be.

You have left the physical world behind and are experiencing the BARDO journey into the spiritual world.

Although the CLEAR LIGHT dawned for you, you were unable to hold onto it.

And when the Secondary Light appeared, you were distracted and it too passed away.

Now you are wandering deeper into the BARDO.

Pay attention to my voice and allow it to guide you through this world of illusions and set you on your course to the Light.

Cling not to the physical world, neither in fondness nor in weakness.

Be not attached to the things or loved ones you left behind.

Call out to your beloved SAVIOR.

Whatever fear or terror or uncertainty comes to you where you are, remember these words for they hold the secret of recognition which will free your Soul —

"Alas! when the Uncertain Experiencing of Reality is
    dawning upon me here,
With every thought of fear or terror or awe for all
    apparitional appearances set aside,
May I recognize whatever visions appear, as the
    reflections of mine own consciousness;
May I know them to be of the nature of apparitions in
    the Bardo:
When at this all important moment of opportunity
    of achieving a great end,
May I not fear the bands of Peaceful and Wrathful
    entities, mine own thought-forms."[25]

(Or make up your own meaningful reminder like above)

Repeat these words whenever visions of awe or terror appear.

Remember their significance as you repeat them and recognition will come to you.

Dear Soul of (name), remember the brilliant Light you glimpsed as your body and mind separated.

That is the radiance of your True Nature. Be not awed nor frightened by it. Recognize it as your True Self.

Remember the sound of a thousand thunders as your consciousness separated from your physical form.

That is the natural sound of your Real Self. Be not awed nor terrified. Recognize it.

Be aware that the body you have now is not of flesh and bones, but a non-material body which cannot be harmed by the images that appear around you.

Recognize that you are in the BARDO.

These are scenes from your life just departed.

Recognize these as your own THOUGHT-FORMS and hold onto the Light through the Love you expressed in your life.

Call out to your beloved SAVIOR and turn toward the Light.

The words of your personal ritual must be in your own language, relevant to your understanding and reflect your personal values and beliefs. The above suggestions include some concepts that may be foreign to you, but they refer to experiences you will only come to comprehend when you go through your death experience and should at least be considered even if they seem strange or weird to you now. There really are no words to describe the wonder of it all, just ask a near-death experiencer to try!

Souls who have not turned to the Light after the third opportunity will find themselves in a place overcast with shadows — dark, ugly, frightening, monstrous shapes which represent their darkest THOUGHT-FORMS. They will experience overwhelming feelings of emptiness and aloneness as if they have fallen into a deep cavern within their own being — into the abyss. The voice of the Reader will be far in the distance and only if they remember to listen for it and concentrate against all odds, will they be able to hear it and climb out of this pit. If not, they will enter the JUDGMENT phase, the FORTY-NINE DAYS OF THE BARDO.

If this section is deemed necessary, the dying person and the Reader will have arranged set times for the twice-daily readings of Part IV. It should be read the first time following Part III.

PART IV

Dear Soul of (name), you have entered the time of Judgment on your journey.

Be aware that you are being pursued by your own past negative qualities.

Recognize the shadows that you see as your own ego passions.

Now is the time to admit your shame and remorse and seek forgiveness by turning towards the Light.

Dear Soul of (name), you cannot escape, you cannot hide, you cannot make a deal.

You now know the effect of your attachments to selfish desires and lustful passions.

You must face the Truth that you now know.

Be not distracted by the energies rising upward through your being.

They are reminders of your passions which got you here, but which can be transmuted. Recognize that this is part of your new existence, but be not involved in the ecstasy.

Let them go and seek immersion with the Light. Know that what you are feeling is divine Love and turn to God for its highest expression.

Listen for the voice of your Reader. Call out to your beloved SAVIOR. Search for your symbol of the Light among the shadows.

Ask for forgiveness and you will not walk this lonesome valley alone.

Dear Soul of (name), if you have passed from the shadow world into the hall of mirrors, you are viewing scenes of your past life.

This Judgment is a mirror held up to your naked Soul.

Now you will truly come to know your Self.

You are the judge of your self and are being forced to realize the significance of your own misdeeds, to see your self as you truly are.

Your Soul bears the burden of shame and remorse for your evil thoughts and negative intentions.

Turn to the Light to end your suffering.

Recognize that these are mental reflections and cannot harm you.

Your life review is to teach you what you refused to learn on earth and to prepare you for your next life.

Dear Soul of (name), you still have Free Will. You may choose at any time to free yourself from this state by either seeking the Light or rebirth into the physical world.

We in the physical world wish you what is for your highest good and continue to pray that you turn toward the Light.

Selah! So Be It! Amen!

Postcards From the Edge

Special prayers meaningful to the dying person may be arranged to be said by loved ones preceding death, following death, at the funeral, and thereafter. These may be standard religious prayers or they may be self-generated according to one's personal beliefs and should direct the Soul toward the Light and through the BARDO. Below are two prayers from the 15th Century as examples. Compare how they sound today with the knowledge of the death-rebirth process.

> *Saint Michael Archangel of God, succor us now before the right high Judge. O champion invincible, be thou present now and assist this (name), our brother, which strongly laboureth towards his end, and defend him mightily from the dragon infernal, and from all frauds of evil spirits. O yet furthermore, we pray thee, which art the right clear and much fair shower of the divinity, to the end that in this last hour of life of this (name), our brother, thou wilt benignly and sweetly receive his soul into thy right holy bosom; and that thou wilt bring him in the place of refreshing, of peace and rest. Amen.[6]*

> *When thy soul passeth out of thy body, may glorious companies of angels come against thee; the victorious host, worthy judges, and senators of the holy apostles meet with thee: the fair, white, shining company of holy confessors, with the victorious number of glorious martyrs, come about thee: the joyful company of holy virgins receive thee: and the worthy fellowship of holy patriachs open to thee the place of rest and joy, and deem thee to be among they that they be among, everlastingly.[7]*

<u>J</u>esus

. . . he said "To you it has been given to know the secrets of the kingdom of God; but for others they are in parables, so that seeing they may not see, and hearing they may not understand. Now the parable is this: The seed is the word of god."
(Luke 8:10-11)!

Tying Up Loose Ends

The medical community, knowing nothing of spiritual laws, has determined such things as the moment of death, when organs should be harvested, and disposal procedures for the body on a strictly biological basis. However, taking into consideration the process of physical death-spiritual rebirth, those issues, as well as other activities around the newly deceased, may need to be reconsidered — whether physicians believe in life after death or not. What their patients believe is what is important.

The consciousness is still aware of its physical body and may still be connected to its body by the SILVER CORD for many hours after breathing ceases and the heart stops beating. Moving the body, removing organs, autopsies, embalming, and even family arguments about the will and thoughtless comments by attending medical personnel, police, coroners, or morticians, within a few hours after a death may be detrimental to the consciously departing Soul.

The Heart SEED ATOM does not depart until the ASTRAL form is fully built and, depending on the person's KARMA, this may take anywhere from one to fifteen hours after death. Removing any organs, especially the heart, before this is completed will severely hinder the Soul's progress. An autopsy or final disposition of a body before the SILVER CORD has broken, may even result in the inability of the Soul to rise above the earth plane, perhaps requiring him or her to reincarnate quickly in a debilitated body. Since medical doctors are unable to sense this event, as an

ANUBISIST could, and act appropriately, they are interfering with the Soul's rebirthing process.

This is also the case for those who die violent deaths and bodily mutilation before or after death. Emotions generated at the time of, and immediately following death have an effect on the Soul's journey and future. Death is the time when peace and calmness should prevail for the Soul's benefit. To be completely sure the Soul is free of its body, the body should be kept in a cold room following death for three days. An autopsy or embalming procedures should not begin until after that time[3] and people who want human heart transplants shall have to wait for medical science to perfect the artificial heart.

The Bon Voyage Party

A funeral is a ritualistic ceremony, usually with religious overtones, which has been performed in memory of the deceased, in most cultures since human society came about. In modern times, it is usually done more for the benefit of those left behind grieving than the departing Soul, but considering the BARDO journey and the spiritual rebirth process the Soul is experiencing in the days following death, the emphasis should be on helping the departed through their Soul birthing process — just as one would at a physical birth.

Without a ritual disposition of a body, the affect on Soul progression is to hold it back slightly — on the individual Soul's BARDO journey, it could mean remaining longer than necessary in a suspended consciousness state before it can move on. It could also slow the process of building its spiritual form.

Not only should you prepare a Living Will, make your own funeral arrangements and decide on the method of disposition beforehand, but, just as people now write their own wedding vows, you should write, in your own words, instructions to your departing consciousness for your loved ones and friends to read to you at your funeral ceremony.

Cremation is the preferred method of body disposal because if the SILVER CORD does not detach by itself (because this person has still not accepted that he or she is dead, cannot let go of the material world, or is experiencing some karmic difficulty), it will be severed by the fire. Another reason is that the Soul has no more need of the physical form it has left behind, as resurrection is in a spiritual body following death, but may be hindered in its progress if its body is still around, preserved in a vault in the earth, to remind it of its depravities or even simply because of the habit of attraction. In any case, cremation of the body fully releases the Soul.[3]

While this is usually considered a time of mourning and deep sorrow over the loss of a loved one, it will become a time of joy with the assurance that, our loss aside, for our loved one's Soul, it is a most joyful experience — especially for the person who has prepared him or herself beforehand. For those left behind, it is still a sorrowful occasion and a heart-felt loss, but the time to grieve is after the dying one has passed into the Light.

Ship to Shore

The information in this book is also meant to help those left behind pick up the pieces of their lives sooner after the death of a loved one by helping them realize that their loved one is going about their new life in the spiritual world, just as they must get on with theirs in the physical world — without each other for a while.

Learning to be in psychic contact with each other in life will create a conscious connection, a bridge, which will not be broken by the death of one or the other. The dead may be able to make themselves visible to loved ones to help them both make the adjustment to this separation[20] and to come to them at their dying time to welcome them home to their spiritual life, together once more. Practicing to contact each other in meditation, telepathically, beforehand, will strengthen the connection.

Lucan
*"The gods concealed from men the happiness
of death, that they may endure life."*

Pulling the Plug

When our Soul decides again to dip down into matter and take on human form, it also chooses which portion of past KARMA to bring in with it and *approximately* how long it will remain in body to learn its karmic lessons and accomplish its spiritual goals. The human being has the Free Will to make choices in karmic situations, but cannot override these conditions sent forth via the Heart SEED ATOM.

KARMA involves physical and mental characteristics, as well as life circumstances, which will help a Soul's human *child* learn what it needs to learn for the Soul's spiritual growth. Many people with severe handicaps or disabilities have succeeded in life only because they had so much to overcome. Many people who seem to have it all on the outside, are empty on the inside and create more new KARMA than they dissolve old, in their life-opportunity.

Sometimes the "sin" we committed in a past life was so severely against the standards to which our Soul aspires, we choose to spread the equal and opposite reaction over more than one life-opportunity. It is the process of spiritual development through involution (spiritual to physical) and evolution (physical to spiritual) that our Soul is undergoing.

Sometimes we choose to return in a severely disabled body or with limited mental abilities for one life or we may choose to spread it out with lesser handicaps or minor mental problems over several lifetimes. Another choice would be to be born into an abusive family in one life or into several slightly dysfunctional families over time. Or into an extremely primitive culture or several barely civilized cultures. You may be male in one life, female in the next to learn about balance. You may be one race, religion or nationality in one life, and another in the next to learn more about tolerance and compassion, or that all wars are folly because we are only fighting ourselves. You may have been a perpetrator in one life and come back to experience victimization in equal measure in one life or to lesser degrees over several lifetimes.

By looking at patterns from your past lives, through past-life regression therapy[18], you can come to understand what certain people and circumstances are teaching you about who you are and why you are here. With the knowledge that there is a Higher Source watching out for us, it makes it easier to accept what we cannot change, to find the courage to change the things we can and to develop the wisdom to know the difference, including deciding when to end our physical life.

With the understanding that KARMA is the driving force behind REINCARNATION, as the process of Soul development progresses, new light is shed on ethical and moral issues, such as suicide, euthanasia, physician-assisted suicide, the right to die, abortion, resusitation, and the death penalty.

Those who have been persuaded to believe that we have only one lifetime and it determines our fate for all eternity, are for or against those issues based on that premise. But, esoterically, there is no right or wrong in KARMA; simply an *equal* and *opposite reaction* based on intentions, motivations and attitudes.

We came into this world for specific reasons to accomplish certain goals and we give ourselves a certain
amount of time in which to do it. Many NDErs, including suiciders, report that they were told it wasn't their
time to die, some were told they had more to accomplish or a mission to do, before they could stay, and
were sent back to their bodies.[21] So it seems plausible
that we cannot die before it is time for us to die, or, at
least, before we accomplish our mission on earth; and
that, when we do die, by whatever means, it was time
or we had already learned all our Soul needed us to
learn in that lifetime. This also implies that our "time"
allowed is not to the minute, but that the "cosmic clock"
is less specific and more flexible.

When death is accepted as a necessary step in our
Soul's progression, even though we have emotional attachments to loved ones and are reluctant to leave
them, the ethical and moral concerns become questions about intentions, motivations and attitudes. If
your psychological or emotional intent is to hurt another human being or destroy yourself, you will attract
karmic baggage to yourself. If your motives are from
your heart, you are forgiven and relieved of karmic
attachments. The loss to one who commits suicide is
the CLEAR LIGHT and the opportunity for SALVA-
TION. You guarantee having to come back and face a
life similar to the one you gave up on — with two
exceptions.

If you are terminally ill, whether from disease or
simply old age, or are severely disabled or in constant
extreme pain, and want to end your life by euthanasia
or physician-assisted suicide, the deciding factor is <u>why</u>

you want to end this life. As in any suicide, if it is only to end your suffering, it is the wrong reason. It would likely mean coming back and suffering even more to break through to the lessons you were supposed to learn in this life; perhaps something about maintaining a biological system in peak condition thus preventing disease and early deterioration or developing strength through pain. In the case of a physician-assisted suicide, the doctor is not culpable, karmically, unless they do it because they get some kind of perverse pleasure out of killing people. This is murder, which carries heavy karmic retribution. None of this is to say we don't have the right to die with dignity if disease or disability has severely diminished the quality of our life; however, consciousness-blocking drugs should be avoided. It is the responsibility of the person desiring release to discover higher reasons for seeking spiritual rebirth, to be sure they have accomplished all they came to do, and to connect with their Spiritual Self. As to keeping people, old or young, alive by machines, this interferes with their spiritual progression. In the case of coma, the Soul is held in a suspended state of consciousness. Releasing them will offer their Souls greater opportunities for growth.

Suicide over a failed romance or great loneliness or major financial loss or the feeling that life isn't worth living, will result in a more miserable next life. Suicide for these reasons is a purely selfish act. The transitional experience and guaranteed BARDO journey of a suicider will reflect the mental thoughts of the person leading up to the act. It will be as pleasant or unpleasant as the intentions of the person dictate, and if not cleared during the BARDO, will be carried over as

KARMA into future lives, where similar situations will present themselves and you will be faced again with the choice.

The other exception involves highly evolved, spiritually-minded persons who may choose to exit their physical life-opportunity whenever they feel ready to accelerate their progression on spiritual levels and use the death-opportunity to achieve SALVATION. This choice is usually, but not always, made in older age when this person, knowing that they have dissolved the KARMA they came in with and haven't accumulated any new KARMA, accomplished what their Soul asked of their lifetime, and with the blessings of their Spiritual Self to which they are consciously connected, feels ready to let go of their physical body and move on to the spiritual world for greater Soul growth. It is suicide by strength of Will; removing the consciousness and the lifeforce from the physical body by merging with the CLEAR LIGHT and returning full consciousness to the Soul. This may be accomplished during intense progressive KUNDALINI meditation and may be assisted by an ANUBISIST. The lifeless body is gently and peacefully left behind and there is no BARDO journey, nor any need to return to the physical world — unless they choose to for a short time for a specific reason to help Humanity. It is our task in every incarnation to achieve this state and it may take thousands to reach it. Many people today are preparing themselves to achieve it in this lifetime.

Abortion is neither right nor wrong, but it will generate karmic consequences for the people involved, depending on their intentions, which most likely will be dealt with in their present lifetimes. There are karmic reasons known only to their Subconscious (Soul) Mind that they became involved in circumstances in which they were faced with the choice of whether or not to terminate a pregnancy. Their learning comes through living with their decision.

For the incoming Soul, it means that it may have to go through the process of preparing for rebirth again, however, it will gain some karmic relief from experiencing an aborted rebirth attempt. The Soul doesn't completely link with its body until the Mental SEED ATOM slides down the SILVER CORD to anchor in the pineal gland at physical birth. It is the last SEED ATOM to enter the body. The Soul, however, does not completely link with the personality *before the seventh year.*[3] When a pregnancy is terminated, the other SEED ATOMS (Heart and/or Emotional, depending on the timing of the abortion) withdraw via the SILVER CORD and the fetus is abandoned. The Soul may have needed to learn a lesson of its own or been willing to sacrifice a life-opportunity to teach a lesson to a group of people. The Soul "knew" it would not get to be reborn at this particular time, and may either quickly choose a new set of parents and seek immediate rebirth or may go on with its life in the spiritual dimensions.

The issue of abortion has polarized society on moral grounds; the argument is between the right of a child to be born and the right of a woman to choose whether or not to continue a pregnancy. The moral judgment is that the rights of the unborn child take precedence over the rights of the mother. In the past, if a choice had to be made during delivery between the life of the mother or the life of the child being born, the child won, which set the precedent for the right of the unborn over the born. These were decisions about appropriate human behavior and morals made by human beings with limited understanding about their spiritual existence and higher purpose, and the karmic reasons for the circumstances.

When these issues are looked at from a karmic perspective, they may be seen more rationally, rather than emotionally. From this higher vantage point, we become more discriminating with our Free Will and make better decisions, which dissolve, rather than accumulate, KARMA. Making judgments about others' choices or dictating what's "right" for others, is ego-centered intent and will be returned, karmically. The heart-intention would be to show compassion for those who are faced with these kinds of decisions and to help when and where we can.

Whether or not to resusitate a person who has been in an accident or suffered a heart attack or who dies on the operating table is currently based on prevailing values and medical ethics; however, as discussed previously, we may not be able to die before it is our time to die nor live because a doctor or paramedic thinks they have to do everything to try to save us or because our loved one thinks he or she can't live without us. The decision takes place on higher planes and is not in the hands of medical science. It is karmically destined. But there is always the hope that we who are concerned for the dying person's life can influence their KARMA by our unselfish actions. To try to rescue or save someone is an act of compassion which reaps karmic rewards for the rescuers and whether the victim lives or dies is the result of his or her own karmic journey. None of this means that resusitation or prayers are a waste of time, only that the outcome is determined by the KARMA of all the people involved.

As for the death penalty, keep in mind that our lifetimes are partly karmically defined and partly the result of our own choices, and that karmic judgment is based on our intentions, motivations and attitudes. Everyone involved in a death penalty case is involved for these reasons and will reap what they sow as their drama unfolds. It may well be that the person who is executed overcomes more KARMA – and needed to from past lives whether guilty or not in this life – than the lawyers and judges, who may end up accumulating more if their motivations are self-serving. A guilty person may escape punishment on earth, but he or she will not escape karmic justice during the BARDO journey nor in future lives.

APPENDIX

Breaking the Language Barrier

AKASHIC RECORD

The Soul's memories of all its experiences in every physical incarnation and every spiritual sojourn. *The total of these records compose the stage of evolution one is in as one progresses toward perfectness; holds the picture images of all events, occurrences and knowledge one has accepted and encountered throughout all lives; recognized as a part of the soul-mind construct comparable to a large computer; takes in exactly what it is fed by the conscious mind and feeds back these records into the bloodstream without being noticed until one reaps negation in his life.*[1]

The Soul departing a lifetime with negative KARMA will journey to the Hall of AKASHIC RECORDS for a life review during its BARDO experience. There you will be confronted with picture images from your life just left and be held accountable for your actions. This journey may also be made while in body by accessing the memories in the Subconscious Mind during past-life regression therapy[26] to clear energy blocks and begin to dissolve KARMA through forgiveness and repentance before it makes the BARDO journey a necessary part of your death experience. It is much less pleasant to deal with in the BARDO than with a competent hypnotherapist in this life.

ANUBISIST

A personal assistant in the process of Soul birthing. A professional Reader of the *Traveler's Guide to Spiritual Rebirth*. A highly sensitive, intuitive and empathic being with the psychic ability to perceive the departing Soul, to know when to remind the Soul about the CLEAR LIGHT and the SAVIOR, and to follow the Soul's progress during the BARDO journey. Adept at teaching KUNDALINI-raising techniques, yogic breathing and meditation. Past-life regressionist and karmic counselor. Probably a near-death experiencer.[18] A highly-evolved Soul.

> When any of likelihood shall die, then it is most necessary to have a special friend, the which will heartily help and pray for him, and therewith counsel the sick for the weal (health) of his soul.[7]

The dying experience is such an overwhelming experience to one who is unprepared that many are likely to miss the opportunities it offers by being so awe-struck or confused they are unable to take advantage of it – thus, the importance of preparatory guidelines and someone to read them to you. And, since not one of us knows exactly when we are going to die, it is also important to prepare for the event by using some of the suggestions in this book to make your transition all that it can be. You can help ease your transition by connecting with an ANUBISIST, who will read from the guidebook (you can write your own specifics according to your own belief system) to your Soul when you make your transition, or by arranging for someone to play a tape recording you made for yourself. There are so many distractions as you shift into the spiritual dimension that even if you have memorized the words, you may forget to say them to yourself in the wonder of it all. You may need an earthly guide to remind you to let go and go to the Light and to call out to your SAVIOR as you cross over into the spiritual world until you meet your spiritual guide on the other side.

Even the spiritually-awakened human being needs to be concentrated on seeing the CLEAR LIGHT as death approaches by a soothing voice at their bedside.

But it is most urgent that a Soul experiencing the BARDO be frequently reminded that they are experiencing mental images that are reflections of their own THOUGHT-FORMS and they need to look for the Light and call to their SAVIOR to move on to higher dimensions. Depending on the level of spiritual awareness of the dying person, the reading may need to go on for a few hours to a few months after death. An ANUBISIST will know how long is necessary, anyone else can only guess.

In the case of an unexpected death or one far from home, the reading should begin as soon as the news of the person's death arrives. When a connection between a Reader and a person has been established previously, the Soul will be able to quickly tune in. Anyone who is likely to be overcome with grief by a person's death should not be asked to be a Reader. This would constitute a further distraction to the Soul in transition and possibly hinder spiritual progress.

The author is in the process of developing a training and certification program for people desiring to become ANUBISISTS. If you are interested in the program or in finding an ANUBISIST in your area, please write to:

S.O.U.L. Foundation
P.O. Box 6141
Palm Harbor, FL 34684-0741

ASTRAL-ETHERIC - See ETHERIC-ASTRAL

BARDO

Between two states; the experiences which occur in the period of time when one is dying (to the physical world) and being reborn (to the etheric world); a twilight state of very real events to the dying person.[1]

The meaning of the *Bardo Thodol* (similar to *The Traveler's Guide*) from *The Tibetan Book of the Dead* is *recognition, by seeing and hearing, that hallucinations are apparitional appearances from one's own thoughts, which sets one free into Reality. The aim of Bardo Thodol teaching is to cause the Dreamer to awaken into Reality, free from karmic illusions, in a state beyond phenomena.*[25]

In *The Egyptian Book of the Dead*, the Soul is defined as *that part of man which beyond all doubt was believed to enjoy an eternal existence in heaven in a state of glory.*[8] Esoterically, Soul is *the condensed intelligence in every atom which is conscious of its intelligence, has knowledge of its function, has knowledge of Totality in its entirety, and has the capacity to remember all the frequencies it has vibrated in.*[1] Your Soul projected "you" into matter. Your Soul was projected by an OverSoul or Divine Spirit, your Higher or Greater Self, your Source. Your Soul is your Subconscious mind, your inner guide, that which knows all about you. A Soul is not something you have, apart from yourself, it is *you* at a higher frequency. You are a manifestation of your Soul in the physical, material, third dimension.

Before taking your last breaths, you may become aware of the biological changes that are taking place as your Soul disconnects from its physical form. You may also be so in awe of your newly awakened psychic senses that you take your attention away from the Light and fail to merge with it. It is easy to become distracted by the wonder of it all, even if you thought you were prepared for it. The habit of the waking conscious mind is to try to control any situation, but do not try to impose your will on this experience. Listen to your Reader's words. Neither run towards nor away from the Light, but relax into it. Allow the Light to flow through you and merge with it.

After the SILVER CORD breaks, freeing the Soul
from its physical form, the average person's Soul spends
three days in a death trance or the BARDO. This is a
transitional state of reality and you may not yet be
truly aware that you are dead. Each Soul will be faced
with a unique personal experience based on the life its
physical form lived. At first, you will not be under the
control of your KARMA and the shadow show of your
THOUGHT-FORMS will not have started. You may
still be hovering around your physical form, seeing and
hearing everything that is going on. Gradually though,
shadowy images will begin to appear. Early in the experience, you will see visions resulting from the good
you did in your life; good thoughts, acts of kindness
and compassion, humanitarian and spiritual work.
Gradually you will move on to darker experiences, re-
flecting the bad, the cruel, the inhumane, the depravity. You may not only view scenes, but take part in
them.³

What is important to remember is that the BARDO
experience takes place <u>in consciousness</u>. It is all a reflection of your thoughts and, while it may seem frightening at first, you won't be harmed. The death BARDO
is like wandering around a picture gallery. Each picture presents a scene from your life and you will see
yourself at your best and your worst. You get to watch
the true nature of your being unfold and experience
the full impact of your actions on others and on yourself. *Heart-borne impulses precede brain-borne impulses, which is
why personified forms of sublime human sentiments will dawn first
then give way to lower animal nature.*⁵

You will think you are alone, but you are not. There
is someone there who will help you if you call their

name and recognize them when they come. For this reason, in life, for many people, it helps to accept a SAVIOR or spiritual guide and become familiar with their image. As the scenes of your life unfold, do not try to flee from the horror; it will only intensify. If you want to get through the BARDO quickly, you will have to face the wrong you did and realize the significance of your acts, otherwise, it will *seem* neverending.

In the BARDO, it is not so much *what* you did but *why* you did it that is reflected. That which you desired most now becomes active. You will be shown your mistakes and how *your* choices caused you to miss opportunities to lead a better life. If you sought the Light in life, more will be given. If not, even a small portion that may have unfolded, will be lost. If you didn't practice forgiveness on earth, you will learn to in the BARDO for you will not be released from a scene until you forgive or are forgiven. Here you will learn many of the lessons you should have learned while on earth through forgiveness. The faces and forms that appear to you are your own mental content, whether they be sublime or horrific. In either case, they are not real. They are neither to be feared nor glorified. They are merely reflections of your thoughts, but they are part of you and you cannot escape them. You need to accept them as part of you and let them go.

The spiritually awakened person will not have to go through the BARDO, instead, you will merge instantly upon death with the CLEAR LIGHT. If your desires were to help others, to love others, and to make the world a better place during your lifetime, you will attract strong, spiritual forces to you as you make your transition. The average person will spend a short time, no more than three days, and merge with the Secondary Light; but a person with constant thoughts of evil may spend the full 49 DAYS OF THE BARDO trying to purify his consciousness. Keep in mind that "days" in spiritual dimensions do not equate to 24-hour days on earth but refer to levels of consciousness one must go through.

> As in the embryonic state in the human species, the foetus passes through every form of organic structure from the amoeba to man, the highest mammal, so in the after-death state, the embryonic state of the psychic world, the Knower or principle of consciousness, anterior to its re-emergence in gross matter, analogously experiences purely psychic conditions. In other words, the one physical, the other psychical — the evolutionary and involutionary attachments, corresponding to the 49 stations of existence are passed through.[25]

Only the lowest consciousness will face the JUDGMENT, which features the reflections of their evil THOUGHT-FORMS. It is not the proclaimed burning fires of "hell" but the intense fires of mental purification the Soul must endure until these images are burned away from the consciousness. Hell is not a place, but a state of consciousness. Holding on to hatreds, needs for revenge, desires for worldly things and physical gratification — these are the crystallized THOUGHT-FORMS of one's own guilt that must be purged. You will experience the hell you created for others, you will meet everyone you ever wronged and suffer their sufferings, you will confront those who wronged you and face the test of forgiveness, and you will judge your response to these tests. The idea is not to break the Soul but to build strength. You will only be given what you can endure and learn from; the rest will be worked out over other lifetimes and transitions.[3]

Imagine your worst nightmare with forms and images of unspeakable horrors surrounding you, refusing to go away, refusing to let up, and you'll have some idea of the terror you may experience. Those who have no remorse, who continue to blame God and others, who are so evil that this is the only level at which they vibrate, will remain here for a very long time. If you focused on sexual lust in life and a sexual scene emerges, any attempt to become involved in it will cause immediate rebirth with no time at all on spiritual planes.

Yet even in all this, there is someone there who will help you, if you call their name. You still have a choice. When you finally admit that you are a victim of your own actions, you are ready to progress. At some point, you finally recognize that this hell was created by your own THOUGHT-FORMS and, through forgiving and receiving forgiveness, you let go of your physical desires, and your Soul will be released. You won't be able to vibrate at the higher dimensions for any length of time, however, and will choose to reincarnate quickly to compensate for your previous evil-doings. This often accounts for a lifetime of severe disability, or several lifetimes with limited disabilities and many obstacles to overcome in order to achieve enlightenment during your next Soul-birthing experience, which could mean merging with the CLEAR LIGHT.

CHAKRAS

Seven energy centers of the spiritual body superimposed along the spinal column of the physical body, from the genital area to the brain, centered on the seven major endocrine glands: Root (prostate/uterus),

Naval (spleen), Solar Plexus (liver), Heart (thymus), Throat (thyroid), Brow (pituitary), Crown (pineal). The human goal is to achieve harmony between the physical, the mental, the emotional, and the spiritual bodies by balancing the CHAKRAS through breath work, meditation, nutritional food intake, physical exercise and developing a more enlightened perspective about life. Maintaining emotional stability and mental clarity and striving for spiritual awareness help keep the energy in balance and the body in good health. The goal at death is for the Life Force to leave the body through the Crown CHAKRA; however, it will exit at the level most consistently expressed in life and rise to the level that matches your state of consciousness in your after-death experience.

Much of the current lifewave on earth are concentrated on their lower CHAKRAS (below the waist). Most of their energy is focused on their sexual energy and they wallow in their emotional dramas; however, their Heart CHAKRAS are beginning to open and they are starting to express more Love in their lives than greed. As people become more evolved through the expression of Love, they will activate the more powerful energies in their head centers, finally awakening the God within and reconnecting with their divine nature. This has been the evolutionary process of Humanity as well as of individual Souls on their path toward achieving their full potential as spiritual beings in the Kingdom of God. We are each on our own Path, going at our own speed.

CLEAR LIGHT

A very vivid, dazzling, brilliant white light that human eyes cannot tolerate up close, and yet it gives off no heat; light of pure intelligence; pure Reality, Nirvana, all-there-is.[1] The reflection of consciousness (mirror of the mind) without any limitations or darkness; being in Bliss; Oneness with God; coming face to face with God. *Beyond description; no width, no depth, no height, no center, no color, no weight, no form, no name, no time, no space, no emotion, no action.*[5] The experience of Oneness with that which is beyond consciousness.

The CLEAR LIGHT appears to everyone just prior to physical death and offers the opportunity for SALVATION, or Liberation from the CYCLE OF LIFE AND DEATH. If you fail to recognize the CLEAR LIGHT, you will not have the opportunity for immediate SALVATION again until after you spend some time in the spiritual domain, incarnate again in another physical form, and face death again. It is this knowledge which has been hidden by false religious dogma and misconceptions that has kept human beings from reaching their full potential based on the belief that common people will misuse the Knowledge unless they are properly prepared. Fortunately there are built-in safeguards, primarily that a person with evil in his heart would not recognize the CLEAR LIGHT even if he or she had a picture of it in hand at their death. Such a person would be blinded by the Light and turn away from it. Such a person's vibrational pattern does not match that of the Light. You cannot con your way in. You cannot pretend to be what you're not on the spiritual level. Your Soul is showing!

A sincere spiritual seeker with a pure conscious-ness will experience momentary visions of the CLEAR LIGHT while in body and recognize it when it dawns at death. Opening your consciousness to the CLEAR LIGHT before your death insures that you will recognize it at your death and free your Soul to soar to higher planes. The way to achieve this is through certain meditation and breathing techniques to raise your KUNDALINI energy to your head centers.

If you die still filled with hatred, greed, guilt, venge-ful-ness, lust for material pleasures and things, no matter how spiritually aware you are, you will not recognize the CLEAR LIGHT when it dawns. However, if you are sincerely remorseful for your deeds when you approach death and call out to your SAVIOR, you may recognize the second appearance of the Light during the early stages of the BARDO. Recognizing the Secondary CLEAR LIGHT, which will be considerably dimmer than the first, will dissolve a lot of your KARMA but will not free you from the CYCLE OF LIFE AND DEATH. You may spend a good deal of time enjoying life on spiritual planes, but you will choose to reincarnate again to get it right the next time.

CYCLE OF LIFE, DEATH AND REBIRTH - See REINCARNATION

ETHERIC-ASTRAL

The ETHERIC dimension or vibratory level is the electromagnetic energy which surrounds and is within everything — from the atom to man to the planet to the solar system to the galaxy and beyond. Our ETHERIC Double or Aura is a less dense duplicate of our body, and the electromagnetic field that surrounds the earth is a replica of it. The ETHERIC and the ASTRAL planes both encompass and interpentrate the physical plane. The ASTRAL world is very much like the physical in appearance and activities, but is experienced on a much higher level than the physical. Beings there have at least risen to the point of being able to get along with each other and live in peace. These planes are separated by a thin veil, which underdeveloped physical senses cannot penetrate. It takes concentrated meditation to open this window of the Mind. Just as the physical form develops according to the ETHERIC pattern built by the Soul according the karmic record in the Heart SEED ATOM, the ETHERIC form becomes the perfect duplicate of the physical form — only it has no Mind. It is the battery to the physical form — life force, but not mind force. When the Soul leaves the body at death, it also leaves behind the ETHERIC double. Both are required to express life; neither can exist without the other. The ETHERIC form expresses the Soul's lowest potential, it is up to the physical form to express its highest.[5]

Those Souls who go on to experience the BARDO will do so in their ASTRAL body, in which we travel on ASTRAL planes during sleep and out-of-body-experiences, and which clothes our Soul during this transition. This, however, is still not our highest spiritual form, which takes many incarnations to build. A highly-evolved Soul who merges directly with the CLEAR LIGHT at death will find themselves in a much more rarefied body and environment — to match their higher state of consciousness.

49 DAYS OF THE BARDO - See BARDO

KARMA

The Universal Law of Compensation—as the Bible states *whatever a man sows he shall also reap.* (GAL 6:7) Newton's Third Law of motion says *for every action there is an equal and opposite reaction.* Thermodynamics tells us that *energy cannot be destroyed, but only changes form.* KARMA is the Divine Balancer which maintains universal harmony. On the spiritual level, KARMA is the emotional energy underlying an event and when it is not discharged (by asking forgiveness or by forgiving) it becomes blocked energy. There is no right or wrong in KARMA. There is simply an equal re-action to every action. Whatever you do to someone else, will also be done to you. The law also works in our favor because everything we give, is given back to us — with interest, for it is better to give than to take.

There is no escaping Karmic Justice. Karmic Justice is the return you will receive for your acts of kindness and your acts of depravity during your lifetime. Any *intentional* act against another being will be dealt with in kind, if not in this life-time, certainly during your death experience, and possibly in subsequent lifetimes. It is cosmic payment for everything you do. Goodness will be repaid with heavenly bliss, evil with unspeakable horrors. But what does this really mean?

The greatest challenges for a Soul while living in a material world involve not becoming attached to its pleasures. The task is to overcome the *need* for physical, material things. *Needing* to possess things and other people to make your life meaningful leads to hatred, jealousy, resentment, greed, bigotry, intolerance, self-righteousness, pride, arrogance, superiority, aggressiveness, abusiveness, cruelty, emptiness. These influences on the personality lead a person to act in ways that create further KARMA. When you are aware that you are facing a karmic situation, you become more objective and learn how to handle things in better ways. Having things, including great wealth, is not the problem — *needing* them, lusting after them, making them more important than other people, is. To be too human is to be too self/ego-centered. This greed disease that spreads over the world is holding back the Human Spirit. Not only do you not get to take any of your things with you when you die, but during your transition, all the cruelty you inflicted on others to get your needs met, will be returned to you in equal measure. He who has the most toys does *not* win!

The other need for pleasure every Soul must *overcome* involves the sensations and pleasures of the physical body. That doesn't mean do without, but overcome lustful, carnal, animal desires with Pure Love. Sex can be a beautiful, intimate experience shared by two people who love and respect each other, a mindless act of self-gratification, or a violent act of extreme cruelty and self-indulgence. It is the latter two for which you will suffer in kind during your transition and in reincarnations to follow. Learning to re-direct that powerful sexual energy (KUNDALINI) into creativity not only intensifies pleasure on the physical plane, but raises one to ecstatic spiritual heights while still in body. You can achieve *illumination* or *enlightenment* by striving for contact with your higher consciousness through meditation, by focusing your mind on God. Sexual orgasms are just little delights in comparison to a burst or shower of spiritual light flooding your entire body! This is preparation for merging with the CLEAR LIGHT at death — the guarantee that you will recognize it when it dawns for you.

The Bible says to *first* seek the Kingdom of God and everything will given to you. This doesn't mean drop out of the world, go off to a monastery and spend your life in constant prayer. It means keep the *thought* of God first in your mind. Live your life from the place of love in your heart, forgive others, show compassion in your dealings, be giving and kind. The degree of your inner light will determine when your Soul will be ready to merge permanently with the CLEAR LIGHT.

You will be held accountable by your Soul for the way you lived your life on earth and the KARMA you accumulate will determine your transitional experience, your spiritual form, and the circumstances of your next incarnation.

. KARMA is the energy pattern which creates your genetic inheritance for your next incarnation. You (your Soul) will be the judge of your (lower self's) record, judging your self as you judged others in life and suffering the agony of shame and remorse or reaping the joyful spiritual rewards when you leave your physical body behind. You are always you, no matter what form or environment/dimension you are experiencing at any given moment.

The records of all your thoughts, emotions and deeds are written on three permanent SEED ATOMS which are projected via the SILVER CORD into the physical form by your Soul at your birth, and which exit via the SILVER CORD and return to the Soul at your death. This is your Karmic or AKASHIC RECORD, which provides your life review during the BARDO. It is your Soul's memories of all your past lives. It is the realm of your Subconscious Mind. It takes the form of picture images in consciousness, which will reflect all the good and all the bad you did during your past lifetime. AKASHIC RECORDS are actually vibrational frequencies matching the level of your consciousness which attract similar frequencies to you and allow you to rise (or fall) to similar levels in the spiritual dimensions. They follow you wherever you go, in whatever form you take.

We come into this life with KARMA left over from past lives and create more while we're here. Most of the KARMA we create in this life, we get our comeuppance for in this life, but some of it is so despicable, our consciousness cannot even be purified of it during our BARDO journey — which leads us again to experience rebirth to work it out.

If you want to know if something is "wrong," check with your conscience. Your conscience contains the memory in your Subconscious Mind of past transitional experiences, which tries to warn you away from activities that have created KARMA for you in past lives. If your focus is on increasing your spiritual awareness, you will be more in touch with your inner voice than if your focus is on the material world with all its distractions and you are less likely to repeat the same mistakes you've made in past lives.

In some cases, the way you die will release you from a great deal of past KARMA. If you are the innocent victim of a savage murder or a tragic accident, if you die trying to save someone else or during a heroic act, if you are killed in a war or invasion, you may be repaying a karmic debt. The key is not dying with hatred or resentment in your heart, otherwise you may incur further KARMA.

If you die without forgiving someone who wronged you, the KARMA will follow you to your next life and promises to be a hard lesson. The ability to forgive others is even more important than being forgiven so do not hesitate to begin forgiving others now, including those who have died. If you are having hard times in this life, perhaps you have a long history of being unable to forgive. You could change the course of your whole life by practicing forgiveness now. You have Free Will. You have a choice. If you are sincere and earnest, your efforts and motives will be rewarded. By thus purifying your consciousness before you die, you raise your frequency, which will make your transition easier.

Repenting at the moment of death in the hope of escaping punishment will not fly. Unless repentance is made with sincere and deep remorse, you will only incur more KARMA. Deathbed repentance and death rituals alone are not enough to free you from the CYCLE OF REBIRTH. In order to gain complete Liberation from negative KARMA, you must be able to recognize the CLEAR LIGHT when it dawns and merge with it, but if you die with hatred in your heart, you will not even see the Light. You will not be able to reach its frequency. You will go on to experience the BARDO.

KEY TO LIFE

Nothing in the (physical) world can hurt a person, no death of a loved one, no accident, no environmental catastrophe, no chronic illness, no loss of job or marriage; it is only the attitude one takes toward these experiences that hurts the person (karmic blocks).[1]

The KEY TO LIFE is total understanding that one's whole life is a continuous, progressive, developmental process and existence in a physical form as a Human Being is an integral part of the expanding consciousness of a powerful Spiritual Being — a Being who, in essence, strives to sit at the right hand of God.

A Spirit does not reach its fullest potential until it knows intimately every detail about existence in all levels of space, time, dimension, form, and frequency of light. It learns by projecting parts (atoms) of itself into various dimensions (frequency levels) to have experiences relative to those dimensions, and recalls those projected parts back unto itself to bring new knowledge into its Total Consciousness until Universal Understanding or All-Knowledge dawns, which frees the Souls it projected to return to the loving Spirit which sent them forth. It no longer needs to project Souls and its Souls no longer need to manifest in biological forms.

Life in a physical form is not a punishment but a great joy because it is the only time a non-physical energy field can experience physical pleasures and sensations. In the non-physical world, you may dearly love someone, but it is impossible to touch them, to make love to them, to produce children. For these reasons, it is difficult for a Soul to resist the temptation or desire to return to a physical existence time and again with familiar Souls from non-physical realms as classmates in the School of Life to re-experience these pleasures.

What holds back the spiritual evolution of Humanity is the human brain. While the brain of the Human Being is the most highly evolved on this planet, it is not all that it has the potential to be. It needs a certain spark of illumination to make the next leap forward in consciousness — to reconnect with its Spiritual Nature. Many beings today have been able to open the door to their higher consciousness and are accelerating that mind-brain expansion in others, by their example. They have become more peaceful, tolerant and compassionate toward others. As people change their attitudes toward others they perceive as different and begin to see each Human Being as a Soul-Mate on their own Spiritual Path, instead of as an adversary or enemy to be defeated, greater peace and prosperity will come to Human Civilization on this planet.

KUNDALINI

Divine Fire; Cosmic Fire; Serpent Fire; Opening of the Third-Eye; Saved by Grace; Source of psychic energy; the dynamic coil of psycho-spiritual power (energy) lying dormant at the base of the spine in the Root CHAKRA (sexual organs). Sexual energy transmuted to creativity based on our One-ness with God.

Through persistent prayer or meditation focused on God or a SAVIOR, breathing exercises, CHAKRA balancing (positive and negative forces), and by transmuting sexual energy, KUNDALINI rises up the ETHERIC spinal column producing momentary illumination of God-consciousness when it reaches the head centers. Sustained practice affords more time in the higher spiritual realms while in body and recognition of the CLEAR LIGHT upon physical death. Practice enhances intuition, perception, clairvoyant visions, premonitions and spiritual knowledge. The advantage gained is familiarity and comfort with altered states of consciousness similar to those which we experience while Nearing Death Awareness[2] and during our transition. Those who are focused on their God-Self are able to perform healings and awaken KUNDALINI energy in others for their highest good. While this is common practice among yogis and esoterics, it is something anyone who aspires to achieve may practice and reach some level of accomplishment. One doesn't have to give up one's life, just change your priorities to the extent you are willing. At some point in your lifetime, it will become your #1 priority. Without focus on a Higher Source and Pure Love in your heart, you will not be able to achieve this ultimate experience.

Misuse of KUNDALINI energy can have devastating effects on the body and mind – misuse meaning not centered on God-Love. Improper or inadequate training can cause arrested development. Stirred up only as far as the genital region, it can cause sexual deviancy and perversion. Stuck in the solar plexus region, it causes wrenching emotional problems. Skipping over the heart center to the head centers can bring on mental problems, including psychotic breaks.[24] The misuse of this powerful energy in the past caused knowledge of it to be kept secret from the masses by religious orders. Gopi Krishna calls KUNDALINI *the most jealously guarded secret in history.*[14] Even though it has been known about for over seven thousand years, it has been the exclusive property of a secret few. <u>It is not to be fooled with nor taken lightly.</u> It is the most powerful force in nature for it connects us with The Divine. When KUNDALINI rises to the Crown CHAKRA, it opens a channel to your Higher Self, which sends you a downpouring of God's Grace and illuminates the darkest corners of your mind. It is your God-given right to activate your KUNDALINI energy for this purpose alone. It is God's gift to us.

REINCARNATION

The CYCLE or WHEEL OF LIFE, DEATH AND REBIRTH; *The Life Force of the physical body does not die with the physical body, but goes on living in the etheric world for a period of time and is then reborn on earth, repeating this hundreds of times until the Life Force has perfected itself.*[1] Esoterically, REINCARNATION refers to a Monad (Divine Spark of God) undergoing a perfecting process, or a Spiritual Being becoming Divine, by learning to exist in and understand every dimension of GOD.

Plato teaches that a Soul is constantly perfecting itself to become *an initiate into the diviner Wisdom.*[5] This process involves a Monad projecting itself through all dimensions in order to learn <u>all</u> about them. The Souls it projects in turn project into the physical dimension by manifesting in the form of human beings. It takes many projections or incarnations to learn how to exist in and to understand the dynamics of the physical world, mainly because the physical world is so distracting and the Human Being is so easily distracted!

*He who lacketh discrimination, whose mind is un-
steady and whose heart is impure, never reacheth
the goal, but is born again and again. But he who
hath discrimination, whose mind is steady and whose
heart is pure, reacheth the goal and, having reached
it, is born no more.*

—KATHA UPANISHAD

Pythagorous, 2500 years ago, *taught the doctrine of eternal life—not that we have a Soul but that we are a Soul occupying a body. He taught that this immortal Soul is our very being, and we, for a brief time, inhabit a body, but that body is not us; it is a temporary abode—a vehicle to be used during our incarnation on our way toward our liberation from rebirth.*[5]

In order for a Soul to develop to its fullest potential, it must learn to move through all dimensions of space and time by adjusting its vibrational frequency. The greatest challenge occurs when it manifests form in the physical dimension as a human being. Challenge, because during the process of joining its physical form at the moment of its birth, the fragment of consciousness sent by the Soul into each physical incarnation loses awareness of its spiritual heritage. For its first many lifetimes, the "young" Soul has to figure out how to exist in a lower vibrational dimension — in a restrictive environment encased in skin; and, for many more, it has to acquire increasingly complex survival skills in a changing environment, plus figure out how to get along with crazy relatives, noisy neighbors, politics, high unemployment, crime and higher taxes before it can even start to question why it is on earth to begin with. Besides that, in all these many lifetimes (hundreds, maybe thousands), a lot of negative KARMA is accumulated because the memories of our past lives and spiritual sojourns between them are buried deep in our Subconscious Minds. However, if we knew coming in why we were here and what we were supposed to do, we wouldn't learn anything. It is during your death experience that the memory of the last time you died, that you experienced this before, comes back to you.

The journey to God is merely the reawakening of the knowledge of where you are always, and what you are forever, It is a journey without distance to a goal that has never changed. COURSE IN MIRACLES(53)

Books such as the Bible, the Mahabharata, the Torah and the Qur'an, chronicle the origins of Human Being's struggle to rise above the lower CHAKRA energy and become Enlightened. They are chronologies of the evolution of human understanding about who we are, why we are here, how did we get here and how are we supposed to survive, what is life all about, does life go on after death and is there a meaning behind it all. Human understanding has evolved from primitive cultural superstition through quantum physics. Human consciousness has expanded to awareness of "other" dimensions. Life has been our school.

But when we *think* the physical world is all there is, we easily get caught up in it and become *attached* to it and lose sight of the purpose of our human life—to experience it and learn from it, and rise above it.

Consciousness goes on after the brain dies because mind only uses brain to explore and experience the physical dimension. Destruction of the brain does not end its program. Death releases mind from the limitations of the brain and body to soar beyond the galaxies to continue to exist in different forms in different dimensions of GOD, as Divine Beings. Any single physical incarnation, such as the one you and I are personally experiencing, is but a brief moment in our eternal lives as spiritual children of the One Universal GOD. Socrates taught that *those souls which have freed themselves from reincarnation, who have no further commerce with the body and now enjoy unbounded freedom, these now become genii or spirit teachers, who, as Hesiod says, care for the weal (health) of humanity.*[5]

What this means to you and me is that each of us, in this lifetime, have the opportunity to substantially help our Soul's progress by opening the windows of our minds to the light of understanding — to remembering that we are spiritual beings working on our spiritual progress. By focusing your attention on God or a SAVIOR or a Master Teacher, whatever you believe that to be, during your life, you will gradually expand your consciousness to experience existence in more "heavenly," less dense dimensions. The lower your thoughts sink, the lower the dimensions you will experience.

If you wonder why you have this or that problem, look to what your thoughts dwell on consistently. You will attract the forces that vibrate at the same frequency as your thoughts. Once you come to truly know that you are a highly developed spiritual being, wearing a temporary coat of skin in which to experience and learn about the physical dimension, you open the connection to that higher part of your Whole Self and will receive divine guidance in your daily life. This awareness can lead to Liberation from the CYCLE OF DEATH AND REBIRTH in this lifetime and free your Soul to soar to spiritual heights.

Apollonius (a contemporary of Jesus) wrote to a friend upon the death of his son,

There is no death of anyone but only in appearance, even as there is no birth of any save in seeming. The change from being to becoming seems to be birth and the change from becoming to being seems to be death. But in reality no one is ever born nor does one ever die. it is simply a being visible and then invisible—the former through the density of matter, and the latter because of the subtlety of being — being which is ever the same, its only change being motion and rest.[5]

When you go into the death experience with this knowledge, instead of waiting until you get to the other side for the realization to dawn, you may not need to reincarnate again in physical form—unless you want to, briefly, to help humanity (as do many avatars and saviors). REINCARNATION is the result of accumulating negative KARMA (including not seeing the Light), which keeps your essence from being able to vibrate at higher frequencies in order to exist for any length of time on higher dimensions. You may achieve a certain level of spiritual enlightenment in a lifetime, but still harbor selfish or negative thoughts, which will allow you some amount of time in the spiritual realms, but inspire a need to reincarnate to learn how to overcome these deep-seated, lower-level thoughts and emotions.

It is suggested that at the present level of consciousness of the lifewave on the planet, knowledge about our spiritual existence and purpose for being human will propel many Souls to graduate from the school of earth at the end of this lifetime and many more to "get it" in their next incarnation. The human lifewave will eventually dissolve "hell" by turning toward the Light and "evil" on earth will dissipate. It is the Coming of Christ/Buddah/Muhammed/etc. Spirit/Consciousness to Humanity.

SALVATION

To the Hindu, *union with God . . .* to the Greeks, *health, healing and wholeness . . .* to the Christians, *deliverance from the power and penalty of sins . . .*[1] to the Esoteric, overcoming the earth and material desires in favor of union with God provides the ability to merge with the CLEAR LIGHT at death, which liberates one from the CYCLE OF LIFE, DEATH AND REBIRTH, from the need to reincarnate in human form, and offers the freedom to express the Soul's higher spiritual potential. All are the same, only the words are different. SALVATION may be achieved by merging with the CLEAR LIGHT at the moment of death by dying with a purified consciousness.

The birth of the Christ within, comes to us through the process of self-purification, altruistic service to others and the expression of love and compassion for all. Redemption comes when you unite your self again with your spiritual self and thus are lifted from the Fall. Only then will man become worthy to share immortality with the gods . . . worthy to share the good with God and live forever.

SAVIOR

Symbol of the Light, Son of God, Master Teacher, Saint or Avatar who warrants your highest love, reverence and respect.

When you accept a SAVIOR into your life, you forge a bond or make a connection, or build a bridge that will help you not only in this life, but during your transition to the next. The more you meditate upon some divine being during your lifetime, the more likely you are to recognize them at your deathtime. Calling their name during your time of need, whether during life or during death, will bring them to your side. It is up to you to live a life that merits their assistance, otherwise you may not recognize them when they come. Your vision will be clouded by your dark THOUGHT-FORMS and you may miss many opportunities, both in life and in death.

> *I am the Way, the Truth, and the Light, and no man cometh unto the Father but by me.*
>> JOHN 14:6

> *...whosoever shall call on the name of the Lord shall be delivered.*
>> JOEL 2:32

Anya Foos-Graber, in her book *Deathing*, suggests that calling out your SAVIOR's name during the BARDO is akin to *hitchiking on the already enlightened 'mirror' of a spiritual being*[9] and certainly that is their higher purpose — to reach out a hand and pull you out of the muck.

SEED ATOMS

These three *permanent* SEED ATOMS are, and always have been, *you*. They are you no matter what form or state of existence you are in. They are the seed pattern, or karmic potential, of an individual Soul since the time it first manifested as an individualized Soul. They come with you into every incarnation and they leave with you each time you die. They are your Book of Life as everything about you from every physical lifetime and spiritual existence is written in them. They are your personal AKASHIC RECORD. They carry your inheritance of all characteristics of weaknesses and strengths from your previous incarnations. Everything you have ever done, said or thought is recorded within them. You are not responsible for the sins of your physical fathers but of your self's previous incarnations. The KARMA you carry is encoded into your DNA (genetic potential) by the Heart SEED ATOM at the moment of conception between the sperm and the egg, which will become your new physical form, born of the parents you have chosen to play out your Karmic Pattern. Your physical form develops according to the ETHERIC pattern built by your Soul according to the karmic record in your Heart SEED ATOM.

The Three Permanent SEED ATOMS are the Emotional, the Mental and the Heart. The Emotional SEED ATOM is lodged in the solar plexus area, more specifically, the liver, and is often called the abdominal brain. It contains the record of all your past desires and habits. This KARMA may be changed by your Will. It is the second to enter the forming physical body; it is the first to leave during death.[3]

The Mental SEED ATOM is located in the pineal gland located in the center of the brain. It contains the record of all your thoughts. This KARMA may also be changed by your Will. It is the last to enter the new form at the moment of physical birth; it is the second to exit during the death process.[3]

The Heart SEED ATOM, located in the heart/thymus area, contains the record of everything (physical, emotional, mental and spiritual) since your Soul's beginning. It is the first to enter the new body and causes the "quickening," the heartbeat to begin; it is the last to leave the physical body at the moment of actual death. It ties you to your Karmic destiny and cannot be changed by your Will. Thus we are, at the same time, subject to fate and masters of our fate. However, even to change one's Mental and Emotional KARMA by Will takes transcendental effort — daily prayer, forgiveness, helping others, giving up negative thinking and activities, becoming a truly spiritual person in your every day life.[3]

The SEED ATOMS produce karmic images that flow through the bloodstream and strike the endocrine glands in the body. They may cause illnesses or disabilities or a major disease that will prevent one from pursuing long-sought goals as compensation for previous transgressions.[3] A Soul may choose to take on a karmic burden to accelerate certain opportunities needed for its progression. It may choose one of total disability rather than four lifetimes with less severe afflictions. While science can achieve certain success in treating diseases caused by diet or lifestyle, doctors can have little effect on karmic illnesses, nor can they discern the difference. This is where the person must learn to heal him or herself using alternative healing methods and doing spiritual work. This may not mean recovering from the disease, in medical terms, but coming to terms with it on a karmic level and healing one's Soul. *Whether we like it or not, death brings healing and release through new life of a different sort. Knowing this profoundly helps us, even though death is not our choice.*[20]

SILVER CORD

Like the umbilical cord that connects the developing fetus to its life-sustaining placenta, the SILVER CORD connects the developing human being to is life-sustaining Soul. The umbilical cord transfers sustanence to the fetus from the mother, the SILVER CORD, Life Force from the Soul to its physical form. The umbilical cord is severed at birth, the SILVER CORD severes at death. At severence, just as the fetus goes on to become a human being, the human being goes on to become a spiritual being. *As it is above, so it is below.* Just as the building blocks of the physical form are transmitted via the umbilical cord from the placenta to the fetus, the SEED ATOMS upon which the physical form and personality are to be built travel through the SILVER CORD from the Soul to the united egg and sperm. Upon physical death, the SEED ATOMS return via the SILVER CORD to their origin until activated for another incarnation in the physical world.

THOUGHT-FORMS

The more you think about something, whether good or evil, the more "crystallized" it becomes — it may be glorious and beautiful or monstrous and frightening. These are your own mental visions and constructs taking form. *You are what you think*, so guard your thoughts carefully. Building the proper THOUGHT-FORMS, if not done during your lifetime, takes on great importance in the days preceding death. Since most of us do not have the good fortune of knowing when we will face our own death, it is wise to turn our thoughts to God now. One minute you may be alive and having fun and the next, be dead; therefore, it is never too soon to prepare for this inevitable event in our lives.

In the beginning of learning meditation, it may be very unpleasant as you find yourself face-to-face with your negative THOUGHT-FORMS. You have the opportunity to destroy them by recognizing them as THOUGHT-FORMS—don't try to run and hide, turn and face them with forgiveness and they will disappear and lose their power over you.

When beginning to work with KUNDALINI, the Root CHAKRA is the first to open and all your gruesome sexual thoughts and fears will surface. They may appear to be alive but they are only mental images, they are not real, and they may be dissolved by mentally bringing them into the light during meditation. If this is not done, that which you fear will come to you for you are the one who created the THOUGHT-FORM. Once you have activated KUNDALINI, you must continue to look toward the light — do not stop half-way up the mountain. Surround yourself with White Light (thoughts of God's Love) until the THOUGHT-FORMS dissolve. Eventually, you will destroy them all and your meditations will be free of disturbances, and you will begin to see the Light which you will recognize when you die.

During your transition, the undissolved THOUGHT-FORMS you created in life will determine what you will experience in death. You will experience the THOUGHT-FORMS you created of enemies, loved ones and worshipped idols or deities. You may encounter heavenly visions or nightmares which are the mental reflections of your lower consciousness. You will go where your mind dwells. You will only be able to hold onto the Light to the degree that you formed the *thought* before death.

Plato

"By making the right use of these things remembered from the former life, by constantly perfecting itself in the Mysteries, a soul becomes truly perfect -- an initiate into the diviner Wisdom."

Bibliography

1. BLETZER, June G., Ph.D. *The Donning International Encyclopedic Psychic Dictionary.* Pennsylvania:Whitford Press, 1986.

2. CALLANAN, Maggie and KELLEY, Patricia. *Final Gifts,* NY:Bantam Books, 1993.

3. CHANEY, Earlyne. Astara's *Book of Life* (3rd). California:Astara, 1967.

4. CHANEY, Earlyne. *The Mystery of Death & Dying: Initiation at the Moment of Death.* Maine:Samuel Weiser, Inc., 1988.

5. CHANEY, Earlyne. *Secret Wisdom of the Great Initiates.* California:Astara, 1992.

6. *The Craft To Know Well To Die,* (circa 15th C.), F.M.M. Comper, Ed. London, 1917.

7. *De Arte Moriendi: The Book of the Craft of Dying.* In Bodleian MS. (circa 15th C.), F.M.M. Comper Ed. London, 1917.

8. *The Egyptian Book of the Dead.* E.A. Wallis Budge, Ed. NY:Dover Publications, Inc., 1967.

9. FOOS-GRABER, Anya. *Deathing: An Intelligent Alternative for the Final Moments of Life.* Maine:Nicolas-Hays, Inc., 1989.

10. GOLD, E.J. *American Book of the Dead.* California:Gateways/ IDHHB, Inc., 1990.

11. KUBLER-ROSS, Elisabeth, M.D. *On Death and Dying.* NY:Collier Books, MacMillan Publishing Co., 1969.

12. KUBLER-ROSS, Elisabeth, M.D. *Death: The Final Stage of Growth.* NY:Simon & Schuster Inc., 1975.

13. KUBLER-ROSS, Elisabeth, M.D. *On Life After Death.* California: Celstial Arts, 1991.

14. *Kundalini for the New Age: Selected Writings of Gopi Krishna.* Gene Kieffer, Ed. NY:Bantam Books, 1988.

15. MOODY, Raymond A., Jr., M.D. *Life After Life.* NY:Bantam Books, 1976.

16. MOODY, Raymond A., Jr., M.D. *Reflections on Life After Life.* NY:Bantam Books, 1977.

17. MOODY, Raymond, A., Jr., M.D. *The Light Beyond.* NY:Bantam Books, 1986.

18. MOODY, Raymond A., Jr., M.D. Coming Back: *A Psychiatrist Explores Past-Life Journeys.* NY:Bantam, 1990.

19. MORSE, Melvin, M.D. *Closer to the Light.* NY:Ivy Books/ Ballantine Books, 1990.

20. PARRISH-HARRA, Rev. Carol W. *The New Age Handbook on Death and Dying.* Santa Monica:IBS Press, 1989.

21. RING, Kenneth, Ph.D. *Life at Death: A Scientific Investigation of the Near-Death Experience.* NY:Quill, 1980.

22. RING, Kenneth, Ph.D. *Heading Toward Omega: In Search of the Meaning of the Near-Death Experience.* NY:Quill/William Morrow, 1984.

23. ROSZELL, Calvert. *The Near-Death Experience.* NY:Anthroposcopic Press, 1992.

24. SANNELLA, Lee, M.D. *Kundalini-Psychosis or Transcendence?* San Francisco:Dankin Co., 1981.

25. *The Tibetan Book of the Dead.* Translated by W.Y. Evans-Wentz. NY:Causeway Books, 1973.

26. WILSON, Ian. *The After Death Experience.* NY:Quill/William Morrow, 1987.

If this information has helped you, please buy another copy
and donate it to a library (public, hospital, nursing home,
hospice, school or university). Bless you.

You are invited to send questions and comments to:

Diane Goble
dgoble@BeyondtheVeil.net
Visit my web site at www.BeyondtheVeil.net

==

If you would like more information about Near Death Experiences, contact:

Int'l Association for Near Death Studies (IANDS)
P.O. Box 502
East Windsor Hill, CT 06028 USA
office@iands.org
www.iands.org